Chicago White Sox 2019

A Baseball Companion

Edited by Patrick Dubuque, Aaron Gleeman and Bret Sayre

Baseball Prospectus

Craig Brown and Dave Pease, Consultant Editors
Rob McQuown and Harry Pavlidis, Statistics Editors

Library of Congress Cataloging-in-Publication Data:
paperback
ISBN-13: 978-1-949332-04-9

Project Credits
Cover Design: Kathleen Dyson
Interior Design and Production: Jeff Pease, Dave Pease
Layout: Jeff Pease, Dave Pease

Baseball icon courtesy of Uberux, from https://www.shareicon.net/author/uberux

Ballpark diagram courtesy of Lou Spirito/THIRTY81 Project, https://thirty81project.com/

Manufactured in the United States of America
10 9 8 7 6 5 4 3 2 1

Table of Contents

Part 1: Team Analysis

Part 2: Player Analysis

Part 3: Featured Articles

Foreword

Rob Mains

Welcome to this companion of the 2019 Chicago White Sox. We at Baseball Prospectus are excited to provide this analysis of the White Sox.

Our website, Baseball Prospectus, is a leader in delivering high-quality commentary and data to baseball fans everywhere. To some, those words—commentary and data—appear mutually exclusive. There are people out there who believe that traditional analysis and advanced analytics must run on different paths. But the simplistic narrative of stats vs. traditionalists just isn't true. Every team's analytics department interacts with scouting, development, and major league operations with a common goal: Delivering a championship. New technologies, like radar tracking of pitch speeds and movement, enable talent evaluators to focus on qualitative aspects of pitching like mechanics and pitch sequencing. In-game strategies like infield shifts, based on batters' hit tendencies, help turn balls in play into outs. Hitters use information to adjust their swings to maximize run production.

All these numbers can seem, at best, intimidating, and at worst, counterproductive to the casual fan. Even as technology and analysis have embedded themselves deeply into the way teams run, it can often feel like statistics create a displacement between the viewer and the sport, breaking them out of the action. And yet every fan incorporates the numbers to some degree; stats like batting average and earned run average, so fundamental to how we talk about performance, are actually complicated formulas. They don't bother people because those formulas have become second nature, as easy to translate as the action on the field.

Along the way, new statistics have entered baseball's lexicon. You'll see some of them, like on-base percentage (which measures a batter's ability to get on base via walk, hit batter, or hit), OPS (on-base plus slugging), and average exit velocity (the speed of balls off a hitter's bat) on broadcasts. Others, like DRC+, might well be new to you. Some of them have been well-defined to the public, others haven't. That lack of context has created ambiguity. Fans know that a ball hit 100 mph is scorched, but does that mean extra bases? (Not if it's hit on the ground or high in the air it doesn't.)

For those who are amenable to them, the new statistics can increase the enjoyment and understanding of the game. They can help fans identify when a pitcher is tiring, when a stolen base or a bunt attempt makes sense (and, more often, when it doesn't), or how a team's lineup might be constructed. Websites like Baseball Prospectus add to that understanding by weaving metrics into the narrative of the game. That's the goal of this publication: to take some of the newer, more complicated statistics and make them as intuitive as the ones on the back of old baseball cards.

But you don't need to love analytics to love baseball. The fans at BP who worked together to write this guide are captivated first and foremost by the game itself. We're drawn to Aaron Judge's power, Francisco Lindor's glove, Billy Hamilton's speed and Patrick Corbin's slider and don't need numbers to tell us why they're so mesmerizing. The underlying statistics provide depth to the game that we all love.

We hope you'll find that this guide helps you better understand the White Sox. Our analysts have studied the team's major league personnel and its minor league affiliates to identify their strengths and weaknesses, both the obvious ones and those that only a careful dissection of players' performances—yes, including the data—can reveal. You don't need us to tell you who was good and who wasn't in 2018, but our models and writers can help you project how each player is going to perform this year and beyond, and appreciate the greatness of each new game as it unfolds. As in the sport itself, the human and analytic components combine to generate a deeper overall understanding.

Think back to the first time you saw a baseball game on a high-definition TV. You'd grown familiar with how the game looked and felt on a picture tube. But new TV allowed you to see details that you'd never seen before. That's how advanced statistics work. The game itself is why you're here and why you're buying this. (And, for that matter, why we wrote it.) The statistical measures provide the sharper focus, the detail, the depth of knowledge that you didn't have before, generating an overall superior picture. Enjoy the view.

—Rob Mains is an author of Baseball Prospectus.

Statistical Introduction

Sports are, fundamentally, a blend of athletic endeavor and storytelling. Baseball, like any other sport, tells its stories in so many ways: in the arc of a game from the stands or a season from the box scores, in photos, or even in numbers. At Baseball Prospectus, we understand that statistics don't replace observation or any of baseball's stories, but complement everything else that makes the game so much fun.

What stats help us with is with patterns and precision, variance and value. This book can help you learn things you may not see from watching a game or hundred, whether it's the path of a career over time or the breadth of the entire MLB. We'd also never ask you to choose between our numbers and the experience of viewing a game from the cheap seats or the comfort of your home; our publication combines running the numbers with observations and wisdom from some of the brightest minds we can find. But if you *do* want to learn more about the numbers beyond what's on the backs of player jerseys, let us help explain.

Offense

At the end of this past year, we've revised our methodology for determining batting value. Long-time readers of Baseball Prospectus will notice that we've retired True Average in favor of a new metric: Deserved Runs Created Plus (DRC+). Developed by Jonathan Judge and our stats team, this statistic measures everything a player does at the plate–reaching base, hitting for power, making outs, and moving runners over–and puts it on a scale where 100 equals league-average performance. A DRC+ of 150 is terrific, a DRC+ of 100 is average, and a DRC+ of 75 means you better be an excellent defender.

DRC+ also does a better job than any of our previous metrics in taking contextual factors into account. The model adjusts for how the park affects performance, but also for things like the talent of the opposing pitcher, value of different types of batted-ball events, league, temperature, and other factors. It's able to describe a player's expected offensive contribution than any other statistic we've found over the years, and also does a better job of predicting future performance as well.

The other aspect of run-scoring is baserunning, which we quantify using Baserunning Runs. BRR not only records the value of stolen bases (or getting caught in the act), but also accounts for a runner's ability to go first to third on a single or advance on a fly ball.

Defense

Where offensive value is *relatively* easy to identify and understand, defensive value is … not. Over the past dozen years, the sabermetric community has focused mostly on stats based on zone data: a real-live human person records the type of batted ball and estimated landing location, and models are created that give expected outs. From there, you can compare fielders' actual outs to those expected ones. Simple, right?

Unfortunately, zone data has two major issues. First, zone data is recorded by commercial data providers who keep the raw data private unless you pay for it. (All the statistics we build in this book and on our website use public data as inputs.) That hurts our ability to test assumptions or duplicate results. Second, over the years it has become apparent that there's quite a bit of "noise" in zone-based fielding analysis. Sometimes the conclusions drawn from zone data don't hold up to scrutiny, and sometimes the different data provided by different providers don't look anything alike, giving wildly different results. Sometimes the hard-working professional stringers or scorers might unknowingly inflict unconscious bias into the mix: for example good fielders will often be credited with more expected outs despite the data, and ballparks with high press boxes tend to score more line drives than ones with a lower press box.

Enter our Fielding Runs Above Average (FRAA). For most positions, FRAA is built from play-by-play data, which allows us to avoid the subjectivity found in many other fielding metrics. The idea is this: count how many fielding plays are made by a given player and compare that to expected plays for an average fielder at their position (based on pitcher ground-ball tendencies and batter handedness). Then we adjust for park and base-out situations.

When it comes to catchers, our methodology is a little different thanks to the laundry list of responsibilities they're tasked with beyond just, well, catching and throwing the ball. By now you've probably heard about "framing" or the art of making umpires more likely to call balls outside the strike zone for strikes. To put this into one tidy number, we incorporate pitch tracking data (for the years it exists) and adjust for important factors like pitcher, umpire, batter, and home-field advantage using a mixed-model approach. This grants us a number for how many strikes the catcher is personally adding to (or subtracting from) his pitchers' performance … which we then convert to runs added or lost using linear weights.

Framing is one of the biggest parts of determining catcher value, but we also take into account blocking balls from going past, whether a scorer deems it a passed ball or a wild pitch. We use a similar approach–one that really benefits from the pitch tracking data that tells us what ends up in the dirt and what doesn't. We also include a catcher's ability to prevent stolen bases and how well they field balls in play, and *finally* we come up with our FRAA for catchers.

Pitching

Both pitching and fielding make up the half of baseball that isn't run scoring: run prevention. Separating pitching from fielding is a tough task, and most recent pitching analysis has branched off from Voros McCracken's famous (and controversial) statement, "There is little if any difference among major-league pitchers in their ability to prevent hits on balls hit in the field of play." The research of the analytic community has validated this to some extent, and there are a host of "defense-independent" pitching measures that have been developed to try and extricate the effect of the defense behind a hurler from the pitcher's work.

Our solution to this quandry is Deserved Run Average (DRA), our core pitching metric. DRA looks like earned run average (ERA), the tried-and-true pitching stat you've seen on every baseball broadcast or box score from the past century, but it's very different. To start, DRA takes an event-by-event look at what the pitchers does, and adjusts the value of that event based on different environmental factors like park, batter, catcher, umpire, base-out situation, run differential, inning, defense, home field advantage, pitcher role, and temperature. That mixed model gives us a pitcher's expected contribution, similar to what we do for our DRC+ model for hitters and FRAA model for catchers. (Oh, and we also consider the pitcher's effect on basestealing and on balls getting past the catcher.)

It's important to note that DRA is set to the scale of runs allowed per nine innings (RA9) instead of ERA, which makes DRA's scale slightly higher than ERA's. The reason for this is because ERA tends to overrate three types of pitchers:

1. Pitchers who play in parks where scorers hand out more errors. Official scorers differ significantly in the frequency at which they assign errors to fielders.
2. Ground-ball pitchers, because a substantial proportion of errors occur on grounders.
3. Pitchers who aren't very good. Better pitchers often allow fewer unearned runs than bad pitchers, because good pitchers tend to find ways to get out of jams.

Since the last time you picked up an edition of this book, we've also made a few minor changes to DRA to make it better. Recent research into "tunneling"–the act of throwing consecutive pitches that appear similar from a batter's point of view until after the swing decision point–data has given us a new contextual factor to account for in DRA: plate distance. This refers to the distance between successive pitches as they approach the plate, and while it has a smaller effect than factors like velocity or whiff rate, it still can help explain pitcher strikeout rate in our model.

New Pitching Metrics for 2019

We're including a few "new" pitching metrics for 2019's suite of Baseball Prospectus publications, but you may be familiar with them if you've spent time scouring the internet for stats.

Fastball Percentage

Our fastball percentage (FB%) statistic measures how frequently a pitcher throws a pitch classified as a "fastball," measured as a percentage of overall pitches thrown. We qualify three types of fastballs:

1. The traditional four-seam fastball;
2. The two-seam fastball or sinker;
3. "Hard cutters," which are pitches that have the movement profile of a cut fastball and are used as the pitcher's primary offering or in place of a more traditional fastball.

For example, a pitcher with a FB% of 67 throws any combination of these three pitches about two-thirds of the time.

Whiff Rate

Everybody loves a swing and a miss, and whiff rate (WHF) measures how frequently pitchers induce a swinging strike. To calculate WHF, we add up all the pitches thrown that ended with a swinging strike, then divide that number by a pitcher's total pitches thrown. Most often, high whiff rates correlate with high strikeout rates (and overall effective pitcher performance).

Called Strike Probability

Called Strike Probability (CSP) is a number that represents the likelihood that all of a pitcher's pitches will be called a strike while controlling for location, pitcher and batter handedness, umpire and count. Here's how it works: on each pitch, our model determines how many times (out of 100) that a similar pitch was called for a strike given those factors mentioned above, and when normalized for each batter's strike zone. Then we average the CSP for all pitches thrown by a pitcher in a season, and that gives us the yearly CSP percentage you see in the stats boxes.

As you might imagine, pitchers with a higher CSP are more likely to work in the zone, where pitchers with a lower CSP are likely locating their pitches outside the normal strike zone, for better or for worse.

Projections

Many of you aren't turning to this book just for a look at what a player has done, but for a look at what a player is going to do: the PECOTA projections. PECOTA, initially developed by Nate Silver (who has moved on to greater fame as a political analyst), consists of three parts:

1. Major-league equivalencies, which use minor-league statistics to project how a player will perform in the major leagues;
2. Baseline forecasts, which use weighted averages and regression to the mean to estimate a player's current true talent level; and
3. Aging curves, which uses the career paths of comparable players to estimate how a player's statistics are likely to change over time.

With all those important things covered, let's take a look at what's in the book this year.

Team Prospectus

You bought this book to learn more about your favorite (or maybe least-favorite, who are we to judge?) team, so let's talk about them. After a thoughtful preview of the 2019 season, you'll be presented with our Team Prospectus. This outlines many of the key statistics for each team's 2018 season, as well as a very inviting stadium diagram.

First you'll find the Performance Graphs page. The first is the 2018 Hit List Ranking. This shows our Hit List Rank for the team on each day of the 2018 season and is intended to give you a picture of the ups and downs of the team's season, including their highest and lowest ranks of the year. Hit List Rank measures overall team performance and drives the Hit List Power Rankings at the baseballprospectus.com website.

The second graph is Committed Payroll and helps you see how the team's payroll has compared to the MLB and divisional average payrolls over time. Payroll figures are currents as of January 1, 2019; with so many free agents still unsigned as of this writing, the final 2018 figure will likely be significantly different for many teams. (In the meantime, you can always find the most current data at Baseball Prospectus' Cot's Baseball Contracts page.)

The third graph is Farm System Ranking and displays how the Baseball Prospectus prospect team has ranked the organization's farm system since 2007. It also indicates the highest and lowest ranks that the farm system achieved over that time.

We start the Team Performance page with the squad's unadjusted and third-order 2018 win-loss records, presented in divisional context. We then list the three highest performing hitters and pitchers by WARP for 2018. Beneath that are a host of other team statistics. **Pythag** presents an adjusted 2018 winning percentage, calculated by taking runs scored per game (**RS/G**) and runs allowed per game (**RA/G**) for the team, and running them through a version of Bill James' Pythagorean formula that was refined and improved by David Smyth and Brandon Heipp. (The formula is called "Pythagenpat," which is equally fun to type and to say.)

Next up is **DRC+**, described earlier, to indicate the overall hitting ability of the team either above or below league-average. Run prevention on the pitching side is covered by **DRA** (also mentioned earlier) and another metric: Fielding Independent Pitching (**FIP**), which calculates another ERA-like statistic based on strikeouts, walks, and home runs recorded. Defensive Efficiency Rating (**DER**) tells us the percentage of balls in play turned into outs for the team, and is a quick fielding shorthand that rounds out run prevention.

After that, we have several measures related to roster composition, as opposed to on-field performance. **B-Age** and **P-Age** tell us the average age of a team's batters and pitchers, respectively. **Salary** is the combined team payroll for all on-field players, and Doug Pappas' Marginal Dollars per Marginal Win (**M$/MW**) tells us how much money a team spent to earn production above replacement level.

Ending this batch of statistics is the number of disabled list days a team had over the season (**DL Days**) and the amount of salary paid to players on the disabled list (**$ on DL**); this final number is expressed as a percentage of total payroll.

Next to each of these stats, we've listed each team's MLB rank in that category from 1st to 30th. In this, 1st always indicates a positive outcome and 30th a negative outcome, except in the case of salary–1st is highest.

The Team Projections page is intended to convey the team's operational capacity entering the 2019 season. We start with the team's PECOTA projected record for 2019, again in divisional context. The **+/-** column indicates how many more or less wins the team is projected to get than they got in 2018. We then list the three highest projected hitters and pitchers by WARP for 2018. A brief farm system summary follows, with the team's top prospect and number of BP Top 101 Prospects. Finally, we list the key new players and departed players, along with their 2019 projected WARP.

Alex Bregman   3B

Born: 03/30/94   Age: 25   Bats: R   Throws: R
Height: 6'0"   Weight: 180   Origin: Round 1, 2015 Draft (#2 overall)

YEAR	TEAM	LVL	AGE	PA	R	2B	3B	HR	RBI	BB	K	SB	CS	AVG/OBP/SLG
2016	CCH	AA	22	285	54	16	2	14	46	42	26	5	3	.297/.415/.559
2016	FRE	AAA	22	83	17	6	0	6	15	5	12	2	1	.333/.373/.641
2016	HOU	MLB	22	217	31	13	3	8	34	15	52	2	0	.264/.313/.478
2017	HOU	MLB	23	626	88	39	5	19	71	55	97	17	5	.284/.352/.475
2018	HOU	MLB	24	705	105	51	1	31	103	96	85	10	4	.286/.394/.532
2019	*HOU*	*MLB*	*25*	*675*	*96*	*38*	*3*	*23*	*78*	*73*	*107*	*12*	*4*	*.272/.359/.463*

Breakout: 6%   Improve: 52%   Collapse: 5%   Attrition: 2%   MLB: 100%
Comparables: Anthony Rendon, David Wright, Pablo Sandoval

YEAR	TEAM	LVL	AGE	PA	DRC+	VORP	BABIP	BRR	FRAA	WARP
2016	CCH	AA	22	285	172	38.9	.286	1.6	SS(51): -3.4, 3B(11): 1.4	2.7
2016	FRE	AAA	22	83	161	10.0	.333	-1.2	SS(14): 2.1, LF(3): -0.1	0.8
2016	HOU	MLB	22	217	107	9.6	.317	0.5	3B(40): 0.9, SS(6): -0.1	1.1
2017	HOU	MLB	23	626	114	34.7	.311	-1.5	3B(132): 8.7, SS(30): -2.9	3.9
2018	HOU	MLB	24	705	150	72.6	.289	-1.6	3B(136): 5.4, SS(28): -0.4	7.4
2019	*HOU*	*MLB*	*25*	*675*	*125*	*37.3*	*.295*	*0.0*	*3B 7, SS 0*	*4.6*

After the projections page, we share a few items about the team's home ballpark. There's the aforementioned diagram of the park's dimensions (including distances to the outfield wall), a few important biographical facts about the stadium, a graphic showing the height of the wall from the left-field pole to the right-field pole, and a table showing three-year park factors for the stadium. The park factors are displayed as indexes where 100 is average, 110 means that the park inflates the statistic in question by 10 percent, and 90 means that the park deflates the statistic in question by 10 percent.

Following the ballpark page, we have a **Personnel** section that lists many of the important decision-makers and upper-level field and operations staff members for the franchise, as well as any former Baseball Prospectus staff members who are currently part of the organization.

Position Players

After all that information and a thoughtful bylined essay covering each team, we present our player comments. Each player is listed with the major-league team who employed him as of early January 2019. If a player changed teams after that point via free agency, trade, or any other method, you'll be able to find them in the book for their previous squad.

First, we cover biographical information (age is as of June 30, 2019) before moving onto the stats themselves. Our statistic columns include standard identifying information like **YEAR**, **TEAM**, **LVL** (level of affiliated play) and **AGE** before getting into the numbers. Next, we provide raw, unstranslated numbers like you might find on the back of your dad's baseball cards: **PA** (plate appearances), **R** (runs), **2B** (doubles), **3B** (triples), **HR** (home runs), **RBI** (runs batted in), **BB** (walks), **K** (strikeouts), **SB** (stolen bases) and **CS** (caught stealing). Then we have unadjusted "slash" statistics: **AVG** (batting average), **OBP** (on-base percentage) and **SLG** (slugging percentage).

Just below the stats box is **PECOTA** data, which is discussed further in a following section. After that, it's on to a pithy and always-informative comment written by a member of the Baseball Prospectus staff, before we cover more stats.

The second text box repeats YEAR, TEAM, LVL, AGE, and PA, then moves on to **DRC+** (Deserved Runs Created Plus), which we described earlier as total offensive expected contribution compared to the league average. Next, one of our oldest active metrics, **VORP** (Value Over Replacement Player), considers offensive production, position and plate appearances. In essence, it is the number of runs contributed beyond what a replacement-level player at the same position would contribute if given the same percentage of team plate appearances. VORP does not consider the quality of a player's defense.

BABIP (batting average on balls in play) tells us how often a ball in play fell for a hit, and can help us identify whether a batter may have been lucky or not … but note that high BABIPs also tend to follow the great hitters of our time, as well as speedy singles hitters who put the ball on the ground.

The next item is **BRR** (Baserunning Runs), which covers all of a player's baserunning accomplishments which includes (but isn't limited to) swiped bags and failed attempts. Next is **FRAA** (Fielding Runs Above Average), which also includes the number of games previously played at each position noted in parentheses. Multi-position players have only their two most frequent positions listed here, but their total FRAA number reflects all positions played.

Our last column here is **WARP** (Wins Above Replacement Player). WARP estimates the total value of a player, which means for hitters it takes into account hitting runs above average (calculated using the DRC+ model), BRR and FRAA. Then, it makes an adjustment for positions played and gives the player a credit for plate appearances based upon the difference between "replacement level"¬–which is derived from the quality of players added to a team's roster after the start of the season¬–and the league average.

Catchers

Catchers are a special breed, and thus they have earned their own separate box which displays some of the defensive metrics that we've built just for them. As an example, let's check out J.T. Realmuto.

YEAR	TEAM	P. COUNT	FRM RUNS	BLK RUNS	THRW RUNS	TOT RUNS
2016	MIA	18935	-8.5	1.8	2.1	-5.6
2017	MIA	18959	5.3	1.7	1.0	9.1
2018	MIA	16399	-0.4	0.9	0.1	0.4
2019	PHI	18448	-1.4	1.5	0.7	0.8

The **YEAR** and **TEAM** columns match what you'd find in the other stat box. **P. COUNT** indicates the number of pitches thrown while the catcher was behind the plate, including swinging strikes, fouls, and balls in play. **FRM RUNS** is the total run value the catcher provided (or cost) his team by influencing the umpire to call strikes where other catchers did not. **BLK RUNS** expresses the total run value above or below average for the catcher's ability to prevent wild pitches and passed balls. **THRW RUNS** is calculated using a similar model as the previous two statistics, and it measures a catcher's ability to throw out basestealers but also to dissuade them from testing his arm in the first place. It takes into account factors like the pitcher (including his delivery and pickoff move) and baserunner (who could be as fast as Billy Hamilton or as slow as Yonder Alonso). **TOT RUNS** is the sum of all of the previous three statistics.

Pitchers

Let's give our pitchers a turn, using 2018 NL Cy Young winner Jacob deGrom as our example. Take a look at his first stat block: the first line and the **YEAR**, **TEAM**, **LVL** and **AGE** columns are the same as in the position player example earlier.

Here too, we have a series of columns that display raw, unadjusted statistics compiled by the pitcher over the course of a season: **W** (wins), **L** (losses), **SV** (saves), **G** (games pitched), **GS** (games started), **IP** (innings pitched), **H** (hits allowed) and **HR** (home runs allowed). Next we have two statistics that are rates: **BB/9** (walks per nine innings) and **K/9** (strikeouts per nine innings), before returning to the unadjusted **K** (strikeouts).

Next up is **GB%** (ground ball percentage), which is the percentage of all batted balls that were hit in the ground, including both outs and hits. Remember, this is based on observational data and subject to human error, so please approach this with a healthy dose of skepticism.

BABIP (batting average on balls in play) is calculated using the same methodology as it is for position players, but it often tells us more about a pitcher than it does a hitter. With pitchers, a high BABIP is often due to poor defense or bad luck, and can often be an indicator of potential rebound, and a low BABIP may be cause to expect performance regression. (A typical league-average BABIP is close to .290-.300.)

After a witty 150ish words on the player like only Baseball Prospectus's staff can provide, it's on to that second stat block, which repeats the YEAR, TEAM, LVL, and AGE columns. The metrics **WHIP** (walks plus hits per inning pitched) and **ERA** (earned run average) are old standbys: WHIP measures walks and hits allowed on a per-inning basis, while ERA measures earned runs on a nine-inning basis. Neither of these stats are translated or adjusted.

DRA (Deserved Run Average) was described at length earlier, and measures how many runs the pitcher "deserved" to allow per nine innings. Please note that since we lack all the data points that would make for a "real" DRA for minor-league events, the DRA displayed for minor league partial-seasons is based off of different data. (That data is a modified version of our cFIP metric, which you can find more information about on our website.)

Jacob deGrom   RHP

Born: 06/19/88   Age: 31   Bats: L   Throws: R
Height: 6'4"   Weight: 180   Origin: Round 9, 2010 Draft (#272 overall)

YEAR	TEAM	LVL	AGE	W	L	SV	G	GS	IP	H	HR	BB/9	K/9	K	GB%	BABIP
2016	NYN	MLB	28	7	8	0	24	24	148	142	15	2.2	8.7	143	47%	.312
2017	NYN	MLB	29	15	10	0	31	31	201¹	180	28	2.6	10.7	239	48%	.305
2018	NYN	MLB	30	10	9	0	32	32	217	152	10	1.9	11.2	269	48%	.281
2019	NYN	MLB	31	13	9	0	31	31	186	145	18	2.3	10.7	221	46%	.286

Breakout: 8%   Improve: 29%   Collapse: 28%   Attrition: 6%   MLB: 85%
Comparables: Erik Bedard, A.J. Burnett, CC Sabathia

YEAR	TEAM	LVL	AGE	WHIP	ERA	DRA	WARP	MPH	FB%	WHF	CSP
2016	NYN	MLB	28	1.20	3.04	3.30	3.5	96.3	59.6	12.1	47.2
2017	NYN	MLB	29	1.19	3.53	3.02	5.7	97.2	55.5	14.5	49.5
2018	NYN	MLB	30	0.91	1.70	2.09	8.0	98.2	52.1	16.3	48.4
2019	NYN	MLB	31	1.02	2.91	3.23	3.9	96.6	54.5	14.8	48.2

Just like with hitters, **WARP** (Wins Above Replacement Player) is a total value metric that puts pitchers of all stripes on the same scale as position players. We use DRA as the primary input for our calculation of WARP. You might notice that relief pitchers (due to their limited innings) may have a lower WARP than you were expecting or than you might see in other WARP-like metrics. WARP does not take leverage into account, just the actions a pitcher performs and the expected value of those actions ... which ends up judging high-leverage relief pitchers differently than you might imagine given their prestige and market value.

MPH gives you the pitcher's 95th percentile velocity for the noted season, in order to give you an idea of what the *peak* fastball velocity a pitcher possesses. Since this comes from our pitch tracking data, it is not publicly available for minor-league pitchers.

Finally, we display the three new pitching metrics we described earlier. **FB%** (fastball percentage) gives you the percentage of fastballs thrown out of all pitches. **WhiffRt** (whiff rate) tells you the percentage of swinging strikes induced out of all pitches. **CS Prob** (called strike probability) expresses the likelihood of all pitches thrown to result in a called strike, after controlling for factors like handedness, umpire, pitch type, count, and location.

PECOTA

All players have PECOTA projections for 2019, as well as a set of other numbers that describe the performance of comparable players according to PECOTA. All projections for 2019 are for the player at the date we went to press in early January and are projected into the league and park context as indicated by the team abbreviation. All PECOTA projected statistics represent a player's projected major-league performance.

The numbers beneath the player's stats–Breakout, Improve, Collapse, Attrition–are part and parcel of the PECOTA projections. They estimate the likelihood of changes in performance relative to the player's previously-established level of production, based on the performance of comparable players:

Breakout Rate is the percent change that a player's production will improve by at least 20 percent relative to the weighted average of his performance over his most recent seasons.

Improve Rate is the percent chance that a player's production will improve at all relative to his baseline performance. A player who is expected to perform just the same as he has in the recent past will have an Improve Rate of 50 percent.

Collapse Rate is the percent chance that a position player's production will decline by at least 25 percent relative to his baseline performance.

Attrition Rate operates on playing time rather than performance. Specifically, it measures the likelihood that a player's playing time will decrease by at least 50 percent relative to his established level.

Breakout Rate and Collapse Rate can sometimes be counterintuitive for players who have already experienced a radical change in performance level. It's also worth noting that the projected decline in a player's rate performances might not be indicative of an expected decline in underlying ability or skill, but could just be an anticipated correction following a breakout season.

MLB% is the percentage of similar players who played in the major leagues in their relevant season.

The final pieces of information are the player's three highest-scoring comparable players as determined by PECOTA. All comparables represent a snapshot of how the listed player was performing at the same age as the current player, so if a 23-year-old pitcher is compared to Bartolo Colon, he's actually being compared to a 23-year-old Colon, not the version that pitched for the Rangers in 2018, nor to Colon's career as a whole.

A few points about pitcher projections. First, we aren't yet projecting peak velocity, so that column will be blank in the PECOTA lines. Second, projecting DRA is trickier than evaluating past performance, because it is unclear how deserving each pitcher will be of his anticipated outcomes. However, we know that another DRA-related statistic–contextual FIP or cFIP–estimates future run scoring very well. So for PECOTA, the projected DRA figures you see are based on the past cFIPs generated by the pitcher and comparable players over time, along with the other factors described above.

Lineouts

In each chapter's Lineouts section, you'll find abbreviated text comments, as well as most of same information you'd find in our full player comments. We limit the stats boxes in this section to only including the 2018 information for each player.

Exclusive Player Visualizations

In our constant battle to provide you with new and interesting baseball content you can't find anywhere else, we've added a trio of data visualizations to each hitter's entry in these books and a pair of visualizations for each pitcher.

For hitters, you'll find three new infographics. The first is each player's **Batted Ball Distribution**, which displays the five major sections of the field: LF (left), LCF (left center), CF (center), RCF (right center), and RF (right). The percentage indicated tells us what percentage of batted balls from that hitter fell within that part of the field during the 2018 season. We've also included the hitter's slugging percentage on balls in play (also called **SLGCON**) for that part of the field.

You'll also see two heatmaps: **Strike Zone vs LHP** and **Strike Zone vs RHP**. These heat maps represent a view of the strike zone from behind the catcher. Areas where there is a darker coloration represent the places where a higher percentage of pitches resulted in hits. In other words, the heatmap represents a hitter's "sweet spots" for getting hits against either left-handed or right-handed pitchers, depending on the image.

Pitchers get two images that help explain what their pitches look like from a hitter's perspective: **Pitch Shape vs LHH** and **Pitch Shape vs RHH**. These images show you the shape and the "tunneling" effect of each pitcher's offerings from the batter's perspective. For each type of pitch that a pitcher throws (represented by an indicator shape), there's a set of dots indicating the flight path, where each dot represents a 0.01-second interval. This maps the average trajectory and speed of an offering, ending where the ball crosses the plate. The solid black box represents the regular strike zone, while the gray contour lines indicate the range of locations that a pitcher typically works in.

Below the image, we provide a bit more detailed information about each pitcher's average offering in the **Pitch Types** box. Here, we also list each of the pitcher's major offerings under the **Type** column.

- **Fastballs** (which usually refers to the four-seam variation)
- **Sinkers** and/or two-seam fastballs
- **Cutters** (which could include "hard" cutters like cut fastballs and "soft" cutters that resemble hard sliders)
- **Changeups** (not including most splitters)
- **Splitters** (split-fingered pitches, forkballs, and some split-changes)
- **Sliders** and/or slurves
- **Curveballs** (including spike-curveballs and knuckle-curveballs, as well as some slurvy curves)
- **Slow curveballs** and/or eephus pitches
- **Knuckleballs**
- **Screwballs**

The **Freq** column indicates the percentage of overall pitches that fall into each of those type categories; if a pitcher has a 16.55% score for changeups, then that's the percent of all pitches that he throws as changeups. **Velo** is exactly what you think it is: the average miles per hour for each pitch type. **H Mov** is the number of inches of horizontal movement on the average pitch of that type, while **V Mov** is the number of inches of vertical movement on the average pitch of that type. (At Baseball Prospectus, we measure this over the long flight of the ball and include gravity into the V Mov number in order to give you the most realistic representation of what the pitch *actually* does.)

If you're wondering about the second number in brackets, that's the index for that velocity or movement compared to the league average. Like DRC+, a score of 100 means that the speed or movement is about the same as league average, while a higher score means that there's higher velocity or movement than the league average. Numbers below 100 indicate less velocity or movement than the league average.

Part 1: Team Analysis

Table for Three: Previewing the 2019 Chicago White Sox

Julie Brady, Nick Schaefer and Collin Whitchurch

How did the team approach the offseason, and did they do well given their aims?

COLLIN WHITCHURCH: Well, I mean, uh…

In all seriousness, this offseason can't be considered anything more than a disappointment. The White Sox had an unbelievable opportunity to vault themselves from rebuilding also-ran to legitimate threat, and they fell flat on their face.

It's not all about their fruitless pursuit of Manny Machado, but it mostly is. Machado would not have single-handedly made the White Sox a World Series threat or even the favorites in their division in 2019, but what better opportunity did they have to improve their roster for both the short and long term, *and* prove they might actually be willing to spend to supplement what they hope to be an exciting young core akin to the one they just blew up than by signing a Hall of Fame talent in his mid-twenties?

NICK SCHAEFER: There's almost too much awfulness to unpack coherently, and it's difficult to know where to begin. If you couldn't land Machado with your payroll at essentially zero and most other bidders sitting on their hands, you're never going to land a free agent of significance. It makes no sense to offer 8/$250 with incentives and options, but balk at 10/$300. The idea of refusing to do an opt-out even though it's clear they're more or less essential at this stage is an arbitrary refusal to acknowledge reality, akin to the pre-hard cap days when the White Sox spent the least in the draft out of spite.

The excuses from Rick Hahn and Kenny Williams are incoherent and contradictory. Williams said they couldn't go to $300 million, but Hahn said their offer stood to make more money for Machado. Then Williams said they couldn't pay it because they had to build a competitive team and they have to pay their rising prospects. If you can't add ~$5 million a year to a $250+ million contract for fear of having too many good players in 8 years—particularly for a player who will almost certainly be worth every penny—then the rebuild looks more like a bait and switch scam rather than a sincere attempt to be more competitive.

The whole thing is a bad joke.

JULIE BRADY: There's not a lot to say that hasn't already been said, or that Sox fans aren't already thinking. Like Collin says, it raises concerns regarding the approach for the future. If the Sox aren't willing to pay for Machado, then who? Are they ever going to sign a great player in free agency? The biggest contract the Sox have ever given out was José Abreu at 6 years, $68 million, and with all the respect that Abreu is rightfully due, that's not superstar money.

It's technically possible that each potential star prospect down in the minors will pan out fully, but that isn't what usually happens. Would the Sox be willing to spend on someone like Nolan Arenado next season, or are they hanging their hopes on Jake Burger and his twice-torn Achilles tendon? Are they banking on being able to draw from their wealth of prospects for trade purposes? It's more concerning when you think of how carefully they've kept Jiménez down for that extra year of control. At some point, they have to spend money to win.

So, after months and months of hearing how serious the Sox were about their pursuit of the two big free agents, it looks like the most probable outcome is they end up with nothing, and no significant additions, again.

NICK: The stars aligned in an unbelievable way and they still messed it up. It's unreal. The whole point of the rebuild was they could not build a winner around some young stars and superstars. Even if they get lucky and this rebuild generates stars, this is a crushing blow to the idea that they can build a winner around the next group.

Even if I have always preferred Harper to Machado, you had a chance to just plop a young, 5+ win player onto the team without sending out prospects to do it and backed out in order to save money a decade from now. Absolutely indefensible.

COLLIN: We could probably spend 10 years and 300 million words re-litigating the White Sox' failed attempt to sign Machado, but we have both respect for our editors and a deadline to hit. Despite our protests, the 2019 season is still scheduled to be played, so let's talk a bit about the players currently on the roster.

Who is your team's breakout player for 2019?

NICK: If I were to describe the broad state of The Rebuild, 2018 represented a really frustrating purgatory instead of providing a sense of clarity or progress, at least at the major league level. Michael Kopech looked good, but had Tommy John—a huge surgery, but not a death sentence. Carlos Rodón made it back from shoulder surgery and looked okay at times, but didn't miss bats. Lucas Giolito and Reynaldo Lopez did nothing to dispel the biggest concerns about them, but nobody has displaced them. Yoan Moncada basically repeated 2017 but for a full year. Do you see any breakouts in this group? Or is what we see what we get with Wave 1 of The Prospects?

COLLIN: I kind of hate being on the positive side of discussions like this because it harkens bad memories of prospects past (Gordon Beckham is going to break out any day now, folks!) but I still believe in Moncada. I think most people are resigned to saying he'll be pretty good, even if he'll never live up to his prospect pedigree, but I still remain bullish that he'll become an All-Star talent. Despite his high strikeout total, Moncada ranked 60th in swinging strike rate out of the 414 hitters who saw at least 500 pitches in 2018, as our Darius Austin noted in his fantasy take last month, and the power and athleticism are still there. Maybe it's "hot take-y" to say a guy who was worth -0.2 WARP in 2018 still has All-Star appearances in his future, but he just seems *so close* to putting it all together, and he's still just 23 with 900 career plate appearances. I expect major improvements in 2019.

As for the pitchers. Well… uh… I think it's time for someone else to talk now.

JULIE: I spent most of last season experiencing the feeling "hope," something so foreign to me as a White Sox fan that my immune system almost rejected it. So I'm really leaning into that to try and dissolve my dark and bitter core, and I feel like I'm higher on some of our pitching options than some people are. Giolito is a good example of this. He had a terrible year! It was very bad. He walked a lot of dudes—90, which was still five off Tyler Chatwood's MLB lead—and gave up a baseball-leading 118 runs over 173 1/3 innings, leading to an… ERA you don't want to see. I'm not trying to argue that there's a way to twist those numbers to make Giolito look like an ace, because, yeesh.

But! Giolito was just 23 years old, pitching in his first full season in the major leagues—he could still be in Double-A at his age and it wouldn't be unusual. Until August, he hadn't even pitched 200 major league innings, total. His fastball isn't necessarily what it used to be, but he has an entire arsenal of offspeed pitches to fall back on. He strikes me as the type of guy who can get lost in his own head while on the mound, but I think that there's still a chance he pulls it all together. I've seen a lot of people completely give up on him, and I think that it's a little too soon to lose faith in someone with as much raw talent as Giolito has, especially given his youth and inexperience.

I've also seen a lot of people write off Rodón too. Look, I get the temptation. The White Sox have been very bad for a very long time, and every time there's an "answer" somewhere—Gordon Beckham, Jared Mitchell, Courtney Hawkins—it feels like it's inevitably followed by disappointment. But, like Giolito, I think it's far too early to pass final judgment on the kind of pitcher Rodón is. He's never really had a chance to stretch out in a full season without injury, and he's still put up very reasonable numbers in the innings he's had. It would be nice to see the strikeouts bounce back—he only had 90 in 120 innings in 2018, his first sub-9.0 SO/9 of his career—and if he can do that, I think he could have a really nice year in 2019.

NICK: I'm glad you made the case for Giolito, Julie. I think Tyler Glasnow has to be the hope there—another former top prospect who is gigantic—Glasnow is 6-foot-8 to Giolito's listed 6-foot-6—who was atrocious in his age-23 season, his first real look at the majors. Turn the page to 2018 and he throws ~110 innings as a roughly league average pitcher split between relief and the bullpen. Giolito would not be the first very tall pitcher to take longer than most pitching prospects to get his mechanics ironed out.

JULIE: Exactly. It's not unheard of, and he's got the physical ability. If he can find some control (famously the world's easiest task) and not overthink it (famously the world's second-easiest task), I think he could really surprise some people.

What player do you see collapsing in 2019?

COLLIN: This is kind of a funny question within the context of the White Sox because most of their players are either young guys coming off of subpar seasons (Moncada, Giolito, Rodón) or fringe roster dudes whose "collapse" would be akin to finding out they're simply not major leaguers (Daniel Palka, Nicky Delmonico, Adam Engel).

There's also Lopez… but again, it's hard to "collapse" when you were worth -0.7 WARP in 2018. However, from a "simple stats" perspective he makes sense, as the reason he was below average by WARP is because his DRA of 5.65 showed him being a much worse pitcher than his 3.91 ERA would indicate. Still, I can't bring myself to buy him as a "collapse" candidate just because a subpar season from Lopez would simply mean those who believe he is destined for relief were proved right.

Then there's Abreu. The 32-year-old is probably your most likely candidate as a plodding slugger on the wrong side of the aging curve. But PECOTA still likes him quite a bit to the point where they see him being worth nearly a full win more than his 2018 All-Star campaign. Players of Abreu's ilk are always at risk of just completely deteriorating seemingly overnight, so he'd probably be my pick if I *had* to choose one. What do you think?

JULIE: The first guy that came to mind was Lopez, but for the reasons above, he's kind of a weird candidate. The second was Anderson, who's another weird candidate. He set a career high in home runs with 20, but also had an OBP of .281 (albeit an improvement over 2017's .276). He stole 26 bases, but he struck out 149 times. It's no question that offensively, he's been making progress, but as hard of a worker as Anderson clearly is, he hasn't shown himself to be a consistently productive hitter yet and that's something the Sox need.

Really, the biggest strides with him happened defensively at shortstop. He's still error-heavy, but errors aren't a great judge of defensive prowess, and even those smoothed out over the course of the season. Short is his, as he declared during the Sox pursuit of a free agent infielder who shall not be named, and hopefully 2019 is the year he has a handle on it from start to finish.

The Sox aren't really in the stage of the rebuild yet where they have players that are established enough to collapse (silver linings!). What I'm mostly worried about is prospects: injuries, regression, retiring from baseball in order to feed their family. Then, when those prospects are finally called up and start performing, *then* is when I will instantly start worrying about their collapse. I can't sleep because what if, in 2020, Jiménez doesn't live up to the expectations set by his upcoming 2019 RoY/MVP campaign?!

NICK: The White Sox have a looooot of fringe major leaguers and those guys have so little margin for error. Ivan Nova pitches to contact, Kelvin Herrera is a reliever trending in the wrong direction coming off his first injury-riddled campaign, Adam Engel's offensive profile hangs by a thread, Castillo is a catcher aging into his 30s… They're all demographics that can implode at any time.

What is your 2019 prediction?

NICK: As we peel the onion of misery that is the Machado Misadventure, we are left staring down the barrel of another bad season. The offseason brought some blandly competent roster filler in Jon Jay and Yonder Alonso, and an upgrade from James Shields at Veteran Innings Eater in Ivan Nova. I'm going to predict that, unlike last year, at least one or two of the Under-25 talents who aren't relievers will break out—I've been a Moncada defender for ages now, I don't plan on stopping yet, for instance.

I think this team winds up winning 73 or 74 games on the back of internal improvement, but there's still disaster potential in the outfield and the rotation.

JULIE: It's wild to think that the season is nigh upon us, especially given that the last couple weeks of the offseason truly felt like Sox fans were getting dragged down an exceedingly long gravel road by Lucinda Williams' car. It's hard to feel good about the upcoming year, but there are definitely things to look forward to.

Regardless of record, this team is going to be less painful to watch than 2018 (an incredibly low bar to pass, to be fair). There are going to be more exciting performances by newly-debuted players (Jiménez! Cease!?), and more room for improvement by the veterans (Moncada! Anderson! Pretty much anyone else!). 2019 is when the next few really intriguing prospects will reach the team (or, at least, have a real shot at doing so), and at its best we'll get a good sneak peek of the better years ahead.

At its worst, though, it'll probably be a slog through a long season. I think PECOTA's 70 wins is a little low, but I wouldn't be surprised if they fall short of 75 either. I'm going to go with 74 wins. But, there's so much room for variance; in a world of peak performance and wild optimism, .500 is tentatively within reach. Dream big!

COLLIN: I wrote last year about how a successful season for the White Sox wouldn't be based on wins and losses but on feeling good at the end of the season about all of the important young players the White Sox were set to roster. Things went miserably and there were virtually no bright spots to be gleaned from the 62-100 season.

This year will be more of the same in terms of expectations. While our Machado-inspired tears have yet to fully dry, there's still a path to feeling good about the 2019 season, and that's one where Moncada and Jimenez look somewhere close to the players prospect watchers believe they can be, Anderson continues to make progress, and Rodón, Giolito, and Lopez make you feel a little better about the possibility that they can succeed in a major league rotation.

All of that can happen in a season where they still win somewhere between 70-75 games and we can still end the season feeling better about ourselves, at least until the offseason comes and we drag ourselves through a process similar to this one all over again.

Eat Arby's.

Performance Graphs

2018 Hit List Ranking

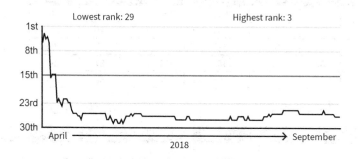

Committed Payroll (in millions)

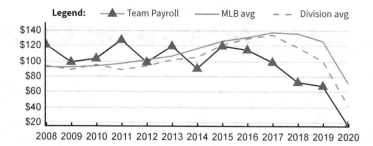

Farm System Ranking

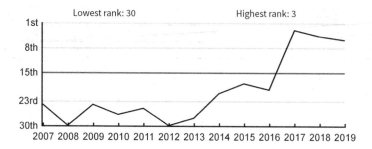

2018 Team Performance

ACTUAL STANDINGS

Team	W	L	Pct
CLE	91	71	.561
MIN	78	84	.481
DET	64	98	.395
CHA	**62**	**100**	**.382**
KCA	58	104	.358

THIRD-ORDER STANDINGS

Team	W	L	Pct
CLE	92	70	.567
MIN	70	92	.432
DET	62	100	.382
CHA	**61**	**101**	**.376**
KCA	58	104	.358

TOP HITTERS

Player	WARP
Tim Anderson	3.8
Jose Abreu	2.3
Avisail Garcia	1.2

TOP PITCHERS

Player	WARP
Jace Fry	1.2
Joakim Soria	0.5
Carson Fulmer	0.3

VITAL STATISTICS

Statistic Name	Value	Rank
Pythagenpat	.381	27th
Runs Scored per Game	4.05	24th
Runs Allowed per Game	5.23	28th
Deserved Runs Created Plus	90	23rd
Deserved Run Average	5.53	27th
Fielding Independent Pitching	4.76	28th
Defensive Efficiency Rating	.708	12th
Batter Age	26.5	1st
Pitcher Age	27.6	11th
Salary	$71.2M	29th
Marginal $ per Marginal Win	$4.3M	13th
Disabled List Days	$834.0M	4th
$ on DL	18%	17th

2019 Team Projections

PROJECTED STANDINGS

Team	W	L	Pct	+/-
CLE	97	65	.598	+6
MIN	82	80	.506	+4
KCA	72	90	.444	+14
CHA	**70**	**92**	**.432**	**+8**
DET	67	95	.413	+3

TOP PROJECTED HITTERS

Player	WARP
Jose Abreu	3.2
Yoan Moncada	2.2
Eloy Jimenez	1.8

TOP PROJECTED PITCHERS

Player	WARP
Michael Kopech	1.6
Carlos Rodon	1.5
Ivan Nova	1.0

FARM SYSTEM REPORT

Top Prospect	Number of Top 101 Prospects
Eloy Jiménez, #4	6

KEY DEDUCTIONS

Player	WARP
Avisail Garcia	1.0

KEY ADDITIONS

Player	WARP
Ivan Nova	1.0
Yonder Alonso	0.8
Alex Colome	0.6
Brandon Guyer	0.4
Jon Jay	0.4

Team Personnel

Executive Vice President
Ken Williams

General Manager
Rick Hahn

Assistant General Manager
Jeremy Haber

Director of Player Development
Chris Getz

Director of Amateur Scouting
Nick Hostetler

Manager
Rick Renteria

Guaranteed Rate Field Stats

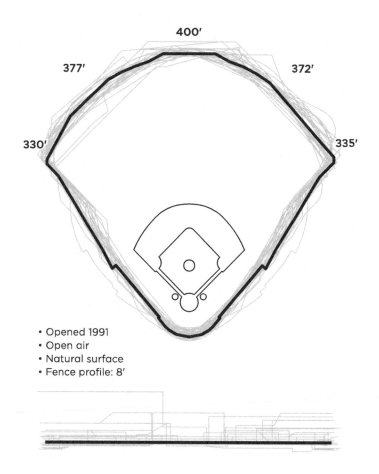

400'

377'   372'

330'   335'

- Opened 1991
- Open air
- Natural surface
- Fence profile: 8'

Three-Year Park Factors

Runs	Runs/RH	Runs/LH	HR/RH	HR/LH
97	97	97	102	110

White Sox Team Analysis

"*Todd's late with the deliverables and Carlos can't get his system running.*" Work anywhere long enough, and the minor snags and hangups that characterize a typical day inevitably snowball into something more. The work was never tedious, and with proper clarity of thought, it still isn't. But after months and years of the same goals, always kept elusive by the familiar impediments, you begin to wonder if there's a better way to spend your day.

"*Chris just chucked Dan's dinner into the whirlpool.*"

Sure, you like your colleagues well enough. But sometimes, too much familiarity breeds contempt. Minor quirks become major personality differences; small interruptions accumulate into unworkable distractions.

"*Yeah, James is here, but, uh, are you sure this is the right guy for this project?*"

Sometimes the new hand can't get anything done.

"*And if I see Avi flail at one more curveball, so help me, I'm going to blow it all up.*"

Avi never stopped flailing at curveballs. And Rick Hahn blew it all up.

⚾   ⚾   ⚾

Jose Quintana and Chris Sale starred together for nearly five years, joined by Adam Eaton and Jose Abreu for the final three. Together, they established themselves as impact players and appeared set to lead the next great White Sox team.

2016 seemed like the long-awaited year. Over the winter, general manager Rick Hahn had bolstered his core with the acquisitions of Brett Lawrie and Todd Frazier. On paper, Hahn finally had a lineup that could keep the team in games on days his aces weren't pitching. For a while, it all clicked. The Pale Hose roared out to a 23-10 start and were six games above second place by mid-May.

It didn't last. Frazier's bat never caught fire, Lawrie regressed, and the incumbent role players did nothing to earn their keep. As Chicago faded, a bad season spiraled into a slapstick routine. Sale made like the Shrike and slashed the team's throwback jerseys ahead of Turn Back the Clock Night. Top prospect Tim Anderson took one walk in the month of July, rekindling a longstanding discussion about the organization's inability to develop young hitting talent.

Chicago traded (now top prospect) Fernando Tatis Jr. for James Shields and the right-hander threw up a 6.77 ERA in 22 starts. The White Sox went 55-74 the rest of the way.

In response, Hahn did what every Twitter egg has begged for since the dawn of the platform, and dove headlong into a full rebuild. That winter, he dealt Sale to Boston and Eaton to Washington. The following July, he shipped Quintana across town to the Cubs.

To many, the moves were a breath of fresh air, the cathartic release that signals the arrival of a new dawn. In a flash, Chicago's long-moribund farm system transformed from one of baseball's worst to among the game's very best. From all appearances, Hahn had masterfully executed his rebuild. His three stars netted Lucas Giolito, Yoan Moncada, Eloy Jimenez, Michael Kopech, Dylan Cease, Reynaldo Lopez, and a handful of other interesting names. Giolito, Moncada and Jimenez were top 10 prospects, per BP's 2017 Top 101 list; Lopez and Kopech graced the top 40, and Cease soon entered their orbit.

It all feels so long ago.

⚾   ⚾   ⚾

It's still too early to call the rebuild a failure, although the preceding statement says much about how things are going. With the benefit of hindsight, it's clear that many of the first-wave prospects were overhyped.

The package for Eaton in particular proved a longstanding prospect axiom: If the return looks too good to be true, it probably is. Analysts covering the deal at the time—the author pleads guilty, your honor—lauded Giolito as the future ace evaluators gushed about in 2015. But by the time of the swap, Giolito no longer resembled that kind of impact talent. He was sitting several ticks lower with his fastball, with much loopier secondaries and only a basic grasp of where anything was going.

Giolito has regressed further in Chicago. He was arguably the worst pitcher in baseball last year, when he led the league in earned runs surrendered and walks allowed. That he also posted one of the lowest strikeout rates among all regular starters seems cruel to mention. At Baseball Prospectus, we annually run a list of the top 10 talents under the age of 26 in each organization as part of our top prospect series. Tellingly, Giolito not only failed to make the White Sox list, but was never part of the discussion.

Moncada did make that list, checking in at No. 2 just behind Anderson. Again though, he doesn't resemble the franchise-altering talent many had hoped for at the time of his acquisition. Moncada is still young and posted adequate numbers as a rookie, but he also proved, at least last year, to be a deeply flawed player.

Every concern scouts had regarding his ability to make contact manifested. He led the league in whiffs—no small feat in 2018—and was also error-prone at second base.

While Giolito looks damaged beyond repair, Moncada is the dystopian avatar for Chicago's rebuild. Despite all his issues with baseball's fundamental components—hitting and catching the ball—the Cuban had his moments last year: He socked 17 homers and produced his share of jaw-dropping highlights. The disconnect should be worrisome for Chicago fans, because it's not that Moncada is *bad*. Despite grizzly WARP and FRAA totals, he clearly has the physical gifts to be a star. Amidst the empty hacks and booted grounders, his periodic successes look like the irrepressible spasms of pure, undistilled baseball talent. Compare his numbers to his raw abilities and you can't help but wonder how Chicago has made so little of so much.

The organization's recent inability to turn baseball protoplasm into steady production lingers like a cloud over the next wave of prospects. Jimenez and Nick Madrigal, the second overall pick in last year's draft, will presumably crack Chicago's lineup in 2019. They are two of the top hitters still loitering in the minor leagues and, as far as prospects go, are very likely to settle in as productive big leaguers. But that last caveat looms large in an organization bereft of recent player development success.

The White Sox haven't produced a consistent, first-division regular in more than a decade (Anderson could conceivably still get there; Avisail Garcia's juiced-ball fueled 2017 campaign may as well have been a dream). Part of that stems from a decades-long reluctance to spend big in Latin America or to splurge for talent in the draft. But the famously-miserly Sox have loosened the purse strings a bit recently and still don't have much to show for it. High-profile picks like Gordon Beckham, Courtney Hawkins and Zack Collins have sputtered in professional ball; toolsy athletes like Trayce Thompson and Marcus Semien have either withered on the vine or blossomed only after leaving town.

All failures point back to a player development operation that has lagged far behind its peers. As clubs throughout baseball spent the last few years experimenting with biomechanical research and the latest radar technology, Chicago's reliance on rote mechanical tinkering and traditional instruction methods was as stuck in the 80s as the red number on Carlton Fisk's left pant leg. The hiring of Chris Getz as director of player development was a breath of fresh air, and under his stewardship the club's development operation has entered the twenty-first century. But this is all more about keeping up with the Joneses than doing anything noticeably innovative, and there's a whole slew of organizational memory that could conceivably stunt well-intended new initiatives; not everyone wants to hear the new guy's pep talk about synergy.

Regardless of any changes at the top, the White Sox need to produce a few success stories before they can shed their reputation as a developmental backwater. Their ability to do so is an existential problem for the franchise—or at least the current administration in charge of it. Regardless of your recent draft picks, financial advantages, or abilities in the trade market, at some point you have to develop *somebody*. All the first-round picks and top prospect acquisitions in the world won't get a team to October if they keep hitting their thirtieth percentile outcomes. And at some point, there won't be a Quintana or Eaton left to flip for the benefit of the next rebuild, when it comes.

For now, a degree of pessimism is warranted in Chicago. If Hahn can't squeeze a good team out of this rebuild, the devastation fans feel will not solely stem from the failure of a promising cadre of prospects, but also from the sense that the organization was too slow to address the systemic problems that led to a rainy decade in the first place; Reds fans know this particular rodeo well. Already, it's fair to second guess the entire strategy.

Since leaving Chicago, Sale has been one of baseball's best pitchers. He's racked up 13 WARP and he very well might have walked home with last year's Cy Young award if he'd been healthy all year. A blown knee has limited Eaton to 120 games—and a footnote in the "what could have been" section of Washington's history books—though he's performed well when available. Quintana, more of a good player than a great one these days, has also been productive since leaving the South Side. Taken together, the group has earned nearly 20 WARP since the moves. Perhaps building around that core, Sisyphussian as it may have seemed at the time, would have provided a more realistic path to contention than trying to do so with volatile prospects and a subpar player development operation.

As the rebuild enters its third year, Hahn's decision must also be examined in the sport's broader economic context. In the past three years, the league's spending and competitive landscape has changed noticeably. The 2016 labor negotiations produced a joint bargaining agreement that, by nearly universal consensus, shifted power toward ownership. In the years since, teams have treated the luxury tax as a firm salary cap. Alongside, they have rushed to cut costs, leading to a depressed free agent market and widespread rebuilding and tanking; last year's American League campaign began with only seven or eight teams seriously trying to compete.

The White Sox, of course, were not one of them. The trades of Sale, Quintana, and Eaton—all of whom had multiple years remaining on team-friendly contracts when they were dealt—augured a period of austerity for the club. Fans of the 2018 White Sox were treated to the spectacle of a team playing in the nation's third largest city running one of the lowest payrolls in the league. Ostensibly, the purpose was to play the kids, and evaluate which players from this crop of rookies have the chops to contribute to the franchise's next competitive team. But the opportunity to strip tens of millions of dollars from the books was surely a pleasant happenstance for the man writing the checks as well.

You can make a case that the White Sox embody much of what is wrong with baseball in 2018. The fire sale (Sale?), the cost-cutting, the empty stadium, the focus on acquiring those sweet, sweet bargain-value prospects even absent a cohesive plan to turn them into major-league ballplayers: it's all here and it's frustrating.

It's all the more frustrating because, lurking beneath the cheap management and player development problems, there really is a decent amount of minor league talent present; the top prospects list at the back of this book sure isn't light on White Sox content. In a weak division, headlined by a Cleveland team that spent the winter openly questioning how much worse they could make their roster while still reaching the playoffs, Chicago isn't *that* far from contention. Develop a couple prize farmhands into solid big-leaguers and augment the roster with a choice free agent or two (there's not a lot of money on the books these days) and this team could theoretically compete as soon as 2020.

2019 will tell us a lot about whether that's realistic. Any development from Moncada and Anderson would be welcome, of course, but it's Jimenez and Madrigal who seem poised to shape the franchise's future. Should they come up and succeed, their arrival could inject life into this dormant franchise. Should that crew falter? Well...

"Rick? This is Mr. Reinsdorf. I would like to have a word with you."

—*Brendan Gawlowski is an editor of Baseball Prospectus.*

Part 2: Player Analysis

Jose Abreu 1B

Born: 01/29/87   Age: 32   Bats: R   Throws: R
Height: 6'3"   Weight: 255   Origin: International Free Agent, 2013

YEAR	TEAM	LVL	AGE	PA	R	2B	3B	HR	RBI	BB	K	SB	CS	AVG/OBP/SLG
2016	CHA	MLB	29	695	67	32	1	25	100	47	125	0	2	.293/.353/.468
2017	CHA	MLB	30	675	95	43	6	33	102	35	119	3	0	.304/.354/.552
2018	CHA	MLB	31	553	68	36	1	22	78	37	109	2	0	.265/.325/.473
2019	CHA	MLB	32	600	73	32	2	22	80	48	114	2	1	.279/.350/.469

Breakout: 0%   Improve: 28%   Collapse: 18%   Attrition: 10%   MLB: 95%
Comparables: Ted Kluszewski, Bob Watson, Derrek Lee

Perhaps to the layman outsider, Abreu's 2018 looks like a classic case of a hulking slugger hitting his thirties and promptly delivering the weakest and most injury-addled season of his proud career. A more uncomfortably insider view would reveal Abreu's strong second half was undone by a pair of injuries (testicular torsion, upper thigh infection brought on by an ingrown hair follicle) that are a bit difficult to link to the everyday wear and tear of salaried baseball. Of course, before all that, he also stumbled into the worst slump of his career fairly organically. Abreu is an odd duck: simultaneously consistent and measured while swinging at nearly everything as a matter of personal preference. His approach is too multifaceted to be relying on any one elite skill, but no more immune to the slow loss of strength and athleticism as anyone else. He will try to play 162 games in 2019, also as a matter of personal preference.

YEAR	TEAM	LVL	AGE	PA	DRC+	VORP	BABIP	BRR	FRAA	WARP
2016	CHA	MLB	29	695	118	21.8	.327	-1.7	1B(152): 7.1	3.0
2017	CHA	MLB	30	675	130	33.1	.330	0.8	1B(139): 5.5	4.1
2018	CHA	MLB	31	553	114	15.1	.294	0.0	1B(114): 4.9	2.3
2019	CHA	MLB	32	600	125	29.7	.317	-0.9	1B 2	3.2

Jose Abreu, continued

Batted Ball Distribution

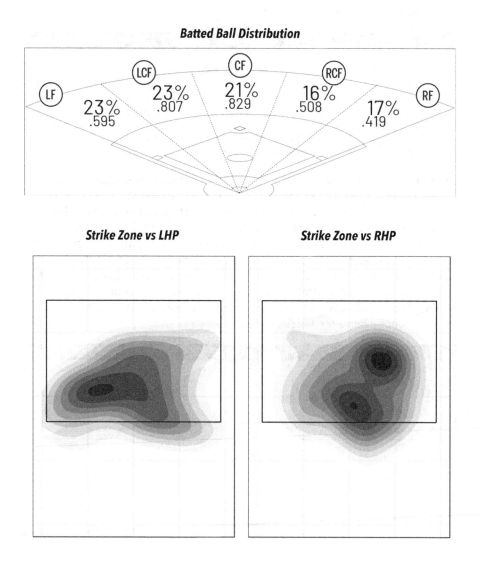

Strike Zone vs LHP   **Strike Zone vs RHP**

Yonder Alonso   1B

Born: 04/08/87   Age: 32   Bats: L   Throws: R
Height: 6'1"   Weight: 230   Origin: Round 1, 2008 Draft (#7 overall)

YEAR	TEAM	LVL	AGE	PA	R	2B	3B	HR	RBI	BB	K	SB	CS	AVG/OBP/SLG
2016	OAK	MLB	29	532	52	34	0	7	56	45	74	3	1	.253/.316/.367
2017	OAK	MLB	30	371	52	17	0	22	49	50	88	1	0	.266/.369/.527
2017	SEA	MLB	30	150	20	5	0	6	18	18	30	1	0	.265/.353/.439
2018	CLE	MLB	31	574	64	19	0	23	83	51	123	0	0	.250/.317/.421
2019	CHA	MLB	32	403	45	19	1	12	49	38	83	1	1	.256/.330/.414

Breakout: 3%   Improve: 29%   Collapse: 17%   Attrition: 12%   MLB: 84%
Comparables: Wally Joyner, Doug Mientkiewicz, Ed Kranepool

After sliding from top-10 pick to middling journeyman, Alonso appeared to enlist in the Launch Angle Revolution in an attempt to violently overthrow our ground-ball overlords in 2017. It worked for the first half, as he suddenly had more game power than he'd shown since the University of Miami. He turned almost all the way back into a pumpkin in the second half, and although he hit 23 homers in 2018, he managed only a .421 slugging percentage that's underwhelming at first base. Worse, his on-base rate, formerly his only asset at the plate, eroded to below league average. The power surge is increasingly looking like a small-sample blip rather than the new normal, which means Alonso is once again a mediocre stopgap.

YEAR	TEAM	LVL	AGE	PA	DRC+	VORP	BABIP	BRR	FRAA	WARP
2016	OAK	MLB	29	532	90	-2.0	.284	0.2	1B(145): 6.5, 3B(7): -0.5	0.7
2017	OAK	MLB	30	371	123	16.8	.301	-0.2	1B(96): -2.7	1.3
2017	SEA	MLB	30	150	125	2.4	.302	-0.1	1B(39): -2.8	0.4
2018	CLE	MLB	31	574	96	8.0	.283	1.1	1B(138): -0.6	0.6
2019	CHA	MLB	32	403	105	10.0	.300	-0.7	1B -2	0.8

Yonder Alonso, continued

Batted Ball Distribution

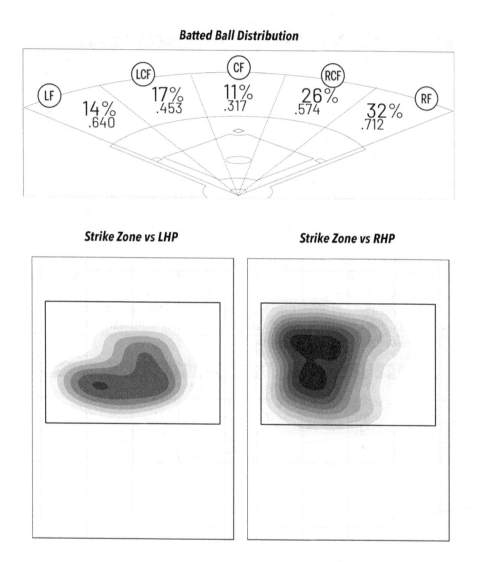

Strike Zone vs LHP

Strike Zone vs RHP

Tim Anderson SS

Born: 06/23/93   Age: 26   Bats: R   Throws: R
Height: 6'1"   Weight: 185   Origin: Round 1, 2013 Draft (#17 overall)

YEAR	TEAM	LVL	AGE	PA	R	2B	3B	HR	RBI	BB	K	SB	CS	AVG/OBP/SLG
2016	CHR	AAA	23	256	39	10	2	4	20	8	58	11	4	.304/.325/.409
2016	CHA	MLB	23	431	57	22	6	9	30	13	117	10	2	.283/.306/.432
2017	CHA	MLB	24	606	72	26	4	17	56	13	162	15	1	.257/.276/.402
2018	CHA	MLB	25	606	77	28	3	20	64	30	149	26	8	.240/.281/.406
2019	CHA	MLB	26	556	66	24	3	16	59	27	138	19	5	.252/.293/.403

Breakout: 10%   Improve: 51%   Collapse: 13%   Attrition: 9%   MLB: 98%
Comparables: Bill Hall, Ian Desmond, Glenn Wright

The typical dog whistle sports radio caller critique, that Tim Anderson is more an athlete than a shortstop of yesteryear, is one the man himself is willing to reverse-engineer. Specifically, after his great leap forward defensively in the second half of 2018, now he feels he has proven himself a shortstop, rather than just an athlete. His profile going forward can be viewed the same way: rather than a collection of tools and upside with an uncertain destination, he has proven he will provide value defending the most difficult spot on the infield, and probably while snagging 20 or more stolen bases in the process. How much his offensive potential will be realized is still an open question after a season of incremental gains over a personally and professionally nightmarish 2017, but it's also less of a big deal. He can pick it.

YEAR	TEAM	LVL	AGE	PA	DRC+	VORP	BABIP	BRR	FRAA	WARP
2016	CHR	AAA	23	256	106	10.9	.384	0.1	SS(52): -1.5	0.7
2016	CHA	MLB	23	431	80	16.6	.375	4.0	SS(98): -4.7	0.8
2017	CHA	MLB	24	606	78	10.6	.328	2.1	SS(145): -11.7	0.1
2018	CHA	MLB	25	606	92	19.9	.289	6.5	SS(151): 9.1	3.8
2019	CHA	MLB	26	556	86	15.9	.310	2.1	SS -3	1.0

Tim Anderson, continued

Batted Ball Distribution

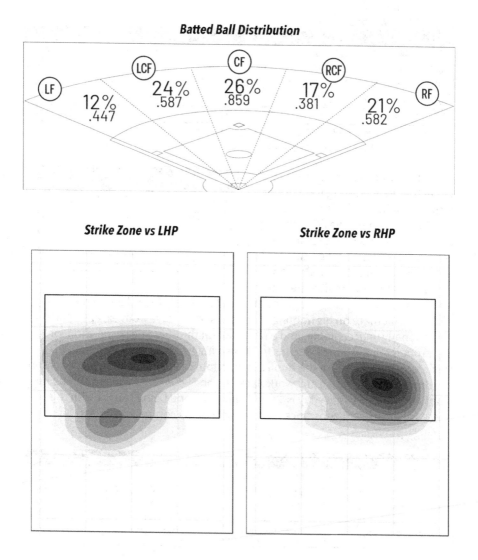

Strike Zone vs LHP

Strike Zone vs RHP

Welington Castillo   C

Born: 04/24/87   Age: 32   Bats: R   Throws: R
Height: 5'10"   Weight: 220   Origin: International Free Agent, 2004

YEAR	TEAM	LVL	AGE	PA	R	2B	3B	HR	RBI	BB	K	SB	CS	AVG/OBP/SLG
2016	ARI	MLB	29	457	41	24	0	14	68	33	121	2	0	.264/.322/.423
2017	BAL	MLB	30	365	44	11	0	20	53	22	97	0	0	.282/.323/.490
2018	CHR	AAA	31	40	2	1	0	0	3	3	11	0	0	.189/.250/.216
2018	CHA	MLB	31	181	17	7	0	6	15	9	46	1	0	.259/.304/.406
2019	CHA	MLB	32	400	44	18	1	13	49	28	105	1	0	.256/.312/.417

Breakout: 5%   Improve: 39%   Collapse: 11%   Attrition: 15%   MLB: 95%
Comparables: John Buck, Ryan Doumit, Nick Hundley

In the final weeks of the season as the White Sox were hurtling toward 100 losses, Castillo—as he is wont to do—hit a little bit. It was nothing life-changing, and his final season line settled in around "OK for a catcher." But when the White Sox reflect on Castillo's failure to provide the veteran

YEAR	TEAM	P. COUNT	FRM RUNS	BLK RUNS	THRW RUNS	TOT RUNS
2016	ARI	15918	-7.7	-1.5	3.1	-6.4
2017	BAL	13481	6.8	1.3	3.2	12.4
2018	CHA	6226	-5.5	-0.8	0.1	-6.4
2018	CHR	901	-0.6	0.0	0.2	-0.4
2019	CHA	15050	-4.4	-0.5	2.1	-2.9

stability they sought in free agency, they will probably focus less on the hitting, perhaps a bit more on his framing numbers' sudden dive from exceptional to exceptionally unacceptable, and a whole lot on the 80-game suspension for erythropoietin and what it means for projecting his role going forward. PED suspensions don't create the ripples in clubhouses for moral and ethical reasons like they used to, but like any workplace, it's one where showing up and being ready to contribute everyday is valued above all, and being caught with this very easily-tested for substance is not a particularly compelling reason for coming up short.

YEAR	TEAM	LVL	AGE	PA	DRC+	VORP	BABIP	BRR	FRAA	WARP
2016	ARI	MLB	29	457	90	18.6	.337	-4.5	C(107): -8.6	0.3
2017	BAL	MLB	30	365	114	20.3	.336	-0.7	C(88): 10.8	3.4
2018	CHR	AAA	31	40	62	-2.3	.269	-0.3	C(8): -0.5	-0.1
2018	CHA	MLB	31	181	93	4.8	.322	0.2	C(43): -6.5	0.0
2019	CHA	MLB	32	400	99	16.8	.322	-0.7	C -6	1.0

Welington Castillo, continued

Batted Ball Distribution

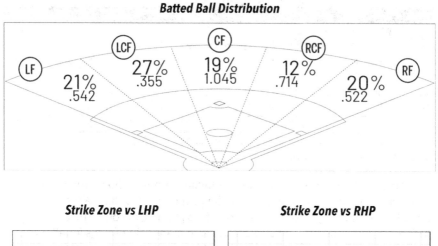

Strike Zone vs LHP   Strike Zone vs RHP

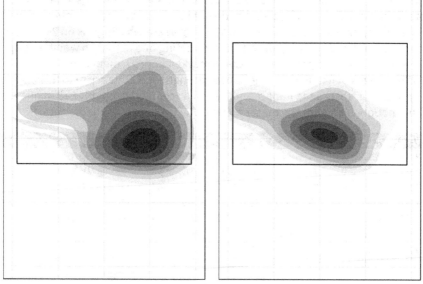

Adam Engel CF

Born: 12/09/91 Age: 27 Bats: R Throws: R
Height: 6'2" Weight: 210 Origin: Round 19, 2013 Draft (#573 overall)

YEAR	TEAM	LVL	AGE	PA	R	2B	3B	HR	RBI	BB	K	SB	CS	AVG/OBP/SLG
2016	WNS	A+	24	64	15	6	1	0	5	7	11	6	0	.327/.413/.473
2016	BIR	AA	24	357	56	18	9	4	25	39	70	31	9	.255/.352/.412
2016	CHR	AAA	24	161	19	6	2	3	16	10	50	8	5	.242/.298/.369
2017	CHR	AAA	25	192	20	12	2	8	19	19	51	4	3	.218/.312/.461
2017	CHA	MLB	25	336	34	11	3	6	21	19	117	8	1	.166/.235/.282
2018	CHA	MLB	26	463	49	17	4	6	29	18	129	16	8	.235/.279/.336
2019	CHA	MLB	27	350	38	12	2	7	30	20	104	12	5	.205/.264/.322

Breakout: 5% Improve: 40% Collapse: 11% Attrition: 14% MLB: 81%
Comparables: Brian Anderson, Jake Marisnick, Leury Garcia

Even Adam Engel grew a little bit tired of talking about his home run robberies by the end of it all. They were three catches out of the 355 that he made during the 2018 season. They are a tiny fraction of his job. Yes, of course he practices them—just a little bit—but he also practices so many other things for all the other days and fielding chances that do not involve anything resembling a home run robbery. Still, if there's a better way to represent why Engel is on 240 major league games and counting despite accumulating one of the ten worst batting lines in baseball this past season—still a marked improvement over 2017—images of him flashing the speed, strength and athleticism to fly into a padded wall, absorb the impact and haul in a scorched deep drive all in one fluid motion, are about the most efficient way to communicate the appeal.

YEAR	TEAM	LVL	AGE	PA	DRC+	VORP	BABIP	BRR	FRAA	WARP
2016	WNS	A+	24	64	161	9.6	.409	3.6	CF(12): -0.9, LF(2): -0.2	0.7
2016	BIR	AA	24	357	110	26.1	.319	5.8	CF(71): -1.8	1.2
2016	CHR	AAA	24	161	75	-0.1	.344	-0.1	CF(25): 4.9, LF(16): -2.1	0.1
2017	CHR	AAA	25	192	92	10.0	.262	1.8	CF(33): -0.3, LF(13): 1.9	0.5
2017	CHA	MLB	25	336	46	-9.3	.247	1.4	CF(95): 7.9, LF(1): 0.0	-0.2
2018	CHA	MLB	26	463	68	-1.1	.322	1.5	CF(140): 10.0	1.0
2019	CHA	MLB	27	350	59	-2.8	.276	1.0	CF 4	0.0

Adam Engel, continued

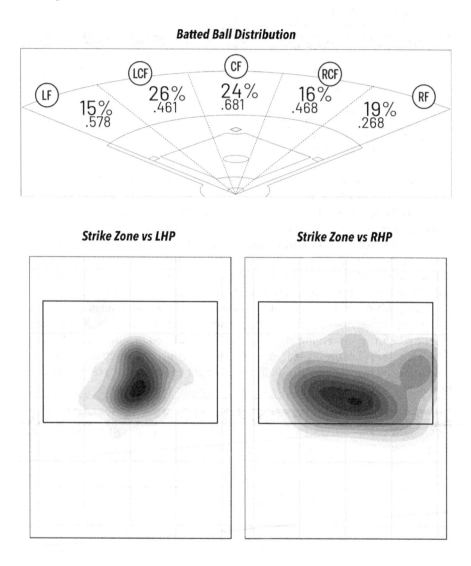

Batted Ball Distribution

LF 15% .578 — LCF 26% .461 — CF 24% .681 — RCF 16% .468 — 19% .268 — RF

Strike Zone vs LHP   **Strike Zone vs RHP**

Leury Garcia   UT

Born: 03/18/91   Age: 28   Bats: B   Throws: R
Height: 5'8"   Weight: 180   Origin: International Free Agent, 2007

YEAR	TEAM	LVL	AGE	PA	R	2B	3B	HR	RBI	BB	K	SB	CS	AVG/OBP/SLG
2016	CHR	AAA	25	342	45	9	4	6	35	24	64	18	8	.313/.367/.426
2016	CHA	MLB	25	50	6	1	1	1	5	1	13	2	1	.229/.260/.354
2017	CHA	MLB	26	326	41	15	2	9	33	13	69	8	5	.270/.316/.423
2018	CHA	MLB	27	275	23	7	4	4	32	9	69	12	1	.271/.303/.376
2019	CHA	MLB	28	296	34	10	2	7	30	18	68	11	4	.255/.312/.386

Breakout: 2%   Improve: 35%   Collapse: 13%   Attrition: 31%   MLB: 73%
Comparables: Eugenio Velez, Freddie Bynum, Matt Szczur

Albeit more subdued in recent years, Garcia was once one of the flashiest dressers in the White Sox clubhouse, flaunting a golden belt buckle that seemed to seek to be as large as his face and another similarly-sized gold plate on his hat to match. His manager—fluent and dexterous Spanish speaker Rick Renteria—refers to him as "Leroy" for reasons unknown. Garcia's most recent tweet was on Aug. 29, where he linked to a Wall Street Journal article about how President Trump's proposed tariffs might affect the Mexican auto industry (Garcia hails from the Dominican Republic). After being one of the worst even-occasional hitters in baseball in 2014 while appearing at seven positions (including pitcher), Garcia mostly disappeared from the major leagues for two seasons, before re-emerging in the opportunity afforded to him in the White Sox rebuild as a serviceable big league utility man. And all of these strange and promising developments surrounding him would be so much more interesting if he could just stay healthy.

YEAR	TEAM	LVL	AGE	PA	DRC+	VORP	BABIP	BRR	FRAA	WARP
2016	CHR	AAA	25	342	119	16.9	.378	1.3	LF(28): 1.2, SS(25): -1.1	1.9
2016	CHA	MLB	25	50	72	-0.4	.294	0.4	CF(16): -1.1	-0.1
2017	CHA	MLB	26	326	82	7.2	.321	0.5	CF(51): 3.4, LF(24): 0.2	0.8
2018	CHA	MLB	27	275	74	5.0	.355	1.8	LF(40): 1.4, CF(26): -0.8	0.3
2019	CHA	MLB	28	296	84	5.1	.310	1.1	2B 0, CF 0	0.5

Leury Garcia, continued

Batted Ball Distribution

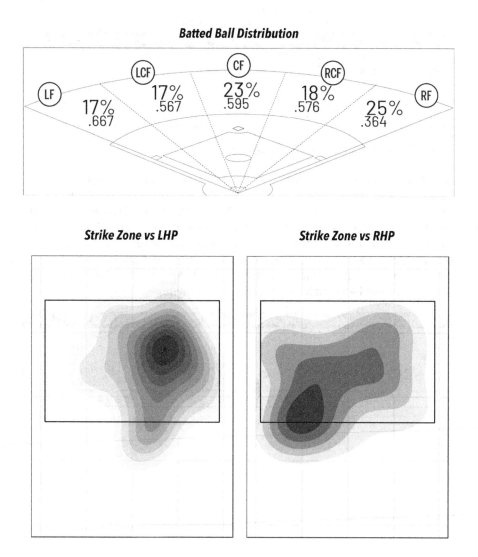

Strike Zone vs LHP   **Strike Zone vs RHP**

Brandon Guyer   OF

Born: 01/28/86   Age: 33   Bats: R   Throws: R
Height: 6'2"   Weight: 200   Origin: Round 5, 2007 Draft (#157 overall)

YEAR	TEAM	LVL	AGE	PA	R	2B	3B	HR	RBI	BB	K	SB	CS	AVG/OBP/SLG
2016	TBA	MLB	30	249	27	12	1	7	18	12	42	2	1	.241/.347/.406
2016	CLE	MLB	30	96	12	5	0	2	14	7	13	1	1	.333/.438/.469
2017	CLE	MLB	31	192	23	7	1	2	20	15	43	2	0	.236/.326/.327
2018	CLE	MLB	32	221	25	11	0	7	27	15	48	1	1	.206/.300/.371
2019	CHA	MLB	33	251	27	11	1	6	27	19	52	2	1	.233/.323/.367

Breakout: 2%   Improve: 25%   Collapse: 15%   Attrition: 14%   MLB: 89%
Comparables: Buddy Lewis, Gregor Blanco, David Murphy

Guyer's non-trivial playing time in 2018 is probably more of an indictment of Cleveland's corner bat options than an endorsement of his current talents. His nice multi-year run is only a few years in the rearview mirror, but modern roster construction squeezes this particular profile — weak-side platoon bats without much defensive utility — harder than pretty much any other. After all, that 17th reliever has to take someone's spot. He still makes enough contact to scoop up playing time for desperate teams or to round out September rosters, but it doesn't look like he's capable of more than that anymore.

YEAR	TEAM	LVL	AGE	PA	DRC+	VORP	BABIP	BRR	FRAA	WARP
2016	TBA	MLB	30	249	119	9.7	.268	-0.8	LF(25): 0.0, CF(18): -0.5	1.0
2016	CLE	MLB	30	96	121	6.4	.379	0.2	LF(26): 2.1, RF(7): 0.1	0.7
2017	CLE	MLB	31	192	81	0.8	.303	0.3	RF(37): 2.5, LF(33): -1.2	0.1
2018	CLE	MLB	32	221	94	-0.7	.237	0.0	RF(76): -1.4, LF(21): -0.3	0.2
2019	CHA	MLB	33	251	91	4.4	.284	-0.1	RF 0, LF 0	0.4

Brandon Guyer, continued

Batted Ball Distribution

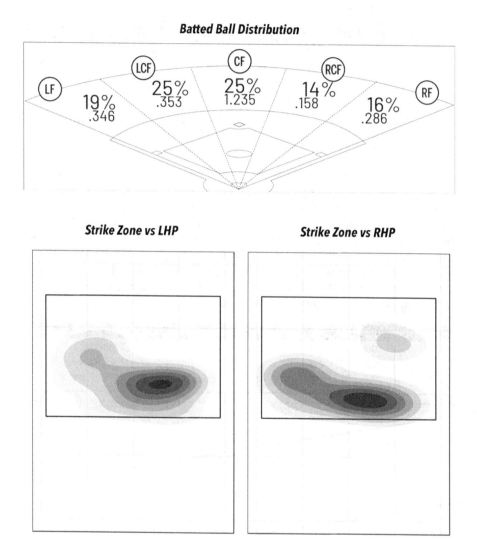

Strike Zone vs LHP

Strike Zone vs RHP

Jon Jay   OF

Born: 03/15/85   Age: 34   Bats: L   Throws: L
Height: 5'11"   Weight: 195   Origin: Round 2, 2006 Draft (#74 overall)

YEAR	TEAM	LVL	AGE	PA	R	2B	3B	HR	RBI	BB	K	SB	CS	AVG/OBP/SLG
2016	SDN	MLB	31	373	49	26	1	2	26	19	78	2	0	.291/.339/.389
2017	CHN	MLB	32	433	65	18	3	2	34	37	80	6	2	.296/.374/.375
2018	KCA	MLB	33	266	28	9	2	1	18	19	39	3	2	.307/.363/.374
2018	ARI	MLB	33	320	46	10	5	2	22	14	56	1	1	.235/.304/.325
2019	CHA	MLB	34	375	36	17	2	4	35	27	77	3	1	.266/.334/.365

Breakout: 0%   Improve: 32%   Collapse: 11%   Attrition: 18%   MLB: 78%
Comparables: Max Flack, Rip Radcliff, Ryan Freel

How was your day? Fine. Did anything exciting happen? Nah, not really. Did you have to manage any conflicts? Nope, things were fine. So your day really was just "fine" then? Yup, just fine. Ok ... This probably isn't exactly how conversations between GMs go when discussing Jay, but you wouldn't blame them if they did. Jay is just fine. He's a lefty batter who doesn't have splits. He's capable of covering center field but doesn't do it exceptionally well. He can get on base a little bit but won't be a major threat on the bases. And the Diamondbacks found this all out first-hand when they traded for him midseason. He's the epitome of just fine, but that's all.

YEAR	TEAM	LVL	AGE	PA	DRC+	VORP	BABIP	BRR	FRAA	WARP
2016	SDN	MLB	31	373	84	18.0	.371	3.1	CF(72): -1.9, RF(9): 0.1	0.7
2017	CHN	MLB	32	433	94	16.7	.368	2.4	LF(64): -3.6, CF(54): -4.8	0.2
2018	KCA	MLB	33	266	80	6.1	.360	-0.5	LF(27): 1.2, CF(15): 1.8	0.3
2018	ARI	MLB	33	320	80	-3.9	.284	-0.1	RF(45): 1.9, LF(14): -1.9	-0.1
2019	CHA	MLB	34	375	89	8.5	.332	-0.3	RF 0, CF -2	0.4

Jon Jay, continued

Batted Ball Distribution

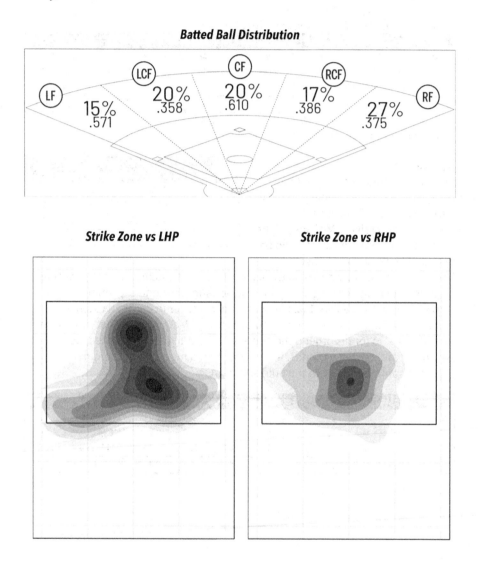

Strike Zone vs LHP   **Strike Zone vs RHP**

James McCann C

Born: 06/13/90   Age: 29   Bats: R   Throws: R
Height: 6'3"   Weight: 225   Origin: Round 2, 2011 Draft (#76 overall)

YEAR	TEAM	LVL	AGE	PA	R	2B	3B	HR	RBI	BB	K	SB	CS	AVG/OBP/SLG
2016	DET	MLB	26	373	31	9	1	12	48	23	109	0	1	.221/.272/.358
2017	DET	MLB	27	391	39	14	2	13	49	26	89	1	0	.253/.318/.415
2018	DET	MLB	28	457	31	16	0	8	39	26	116	0	3	.220/.267/.314
2019	CHA	MLB	29	161	16	7	0	4	16	12	40	0	0	.233/.298/.363

Breakout: 2%   Improve: 49%   Collapse: 7%   Attrition: 15%   MLB: 88%
Comparables: Hank Conger, Tony Cruz, Ronny Paulino

A player who possesses leadership qualities through the roof but can't really hit a baseball is what you'd call, perhaps, a coach? Maybe a GM? Possibly a TED talker? McCann might wish he had a time machine to go back and Kenley Jansen-ize himself,

YEAR	TEAM	P. COUNT	FRM RUNS	BLK RUNS	THRW RUNS	TOT RUNS
2016	DET	13823	3.1	1.1	3.6	8.5
2017	DET	14626	-13.2	-3.4	-0.8	-18.6
2018	DET	16526	-2.3	-1.4	1.1	-2.9
2019	CHA	6112	-2.4	-0.5	0.3	-2.6

because he ranks way down on the list of all sorts of catcher metrics — hitting, framing, blocking, running and also Best McCann. The lone exception: his throwing arm. He was no. 1 last year, the only catcher in baseball to save a whole run with his patent-pending trademarked "McCannon." That run doesn't nearly make up for his other deficiencies, yet he still gets a major-league paycheck, and *that*, my friends, is how you start a motivational seminar (perhaps something else that would suit him).

YEAR	TEAM	LVL	AGE	PA	DRC+	VORP	BABIP	BRR	FRAA	WARP
2016	DET	MLB	26	373	78	-4.3	.283	-2.0	C(99): 5.9	1.2
2017	DET	MLB	27	391	96	13.4	.300	-0.9	C(103): -20.9	-0.5
2018	DET	MLB	28	457	72	-4.8	.282	-4.2	C(114): -5.0	-0.3
2019	CHA	MLB	29	161	85	4.0	.296	-0.4	C -4	-0.1

James McCann, continued

Batted Ball Distribution

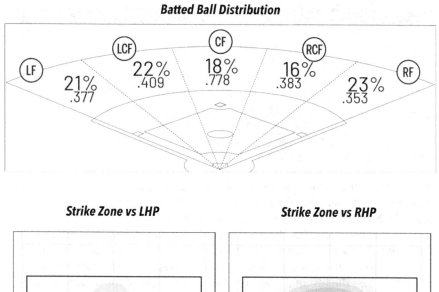

Strike Zone vs LHP

Strike Zone vs RHP

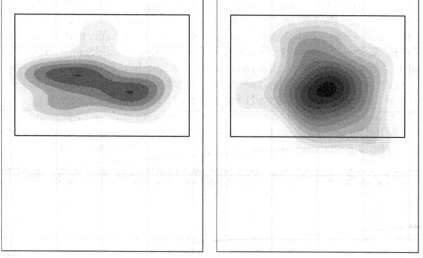

Yoan Moncada   2B

Born: 05/27/95   Age: 24   Bats: B   Throws: R
Height: 6'2"   Weight: 205   Origin: International Free Agent, 2015

YEAR	TEAM	LVL	AGE	PA	R	2B	3B	HR	RBI	BB	K	SB	CS	AVG/OBP/SLG
2016	SLM	A+	21	284	57	25	3	4	34	45	60	36	8	.307/.427/.496
2016	PME	AA	21	207	37	6	3	11	28	27	64	9	4	.277/.379/.531
2016	BOS	MLB	21	20	3	1	0	0	1	1	12	0	0	.211/.250/.263
2017	CHR	AAA	22	361	57	9	3	12	36	49	102	17	8	.282/.377/.447
2017	CHA	MLB	22	231	31	8	2	8	22	29	74	3	2	.231/.338/.412
2018	CHA	MLB	23	650	73	32	6	17	61	67	217	12	6	.235/.315/.400
2019	CHA	MLB	24	630	82	25	4	17	61	64	185	15	7	.235/.317/.386

Breakout: 12%   Improve: 55%   Collapse: 13%   Attrition: 23%   MLB: 94%
Comparables: Javier Baez, Jorge Soler, Mark Reynolds

Judging from interviews, Moncada's 2018 season was at least as confounding to experience as it was to observe. He was so terrible in the first few weeks of the year, which was immediately canceled out by how blisteringly amazing he was at the end of April. It was understandable when he couldn't relocate that rhythm at the plate immediately after a 10-day rehab-less disabled list stint for a minor hamstring strain. It was less so when he couldn't reproduce that power flourish for more or less the rest of the season, and barely avoided the all-time single-season strikeout record. Despite all that, he was never actually bad. You don't lead the league in strikeouts looking without drawing a healthy amount of walks. A strong finishing kick against September pitching helped, and the mental mistakes he made on defense never really threw into question his athletic ability to handle second base. It would have been a suitably promising—if aesthetically grueling—campaign for an athletic 23-year-old middle infield with dizzying tools and a good eye, if that 23-year-old were not former No. 1 global prospect and centerpiece of The Chris Sale Trade.

YEAR	TEAM	LVL	AGE	PA	DRC+	VORP	BABIP	BRR	FRAA	WARP
2016	SLM	A+	21	284	160	32.0	.395	6.2	2B(58): -1.7	2.1
2016	PME	AA	21	207	128	16.4	.373	0.6	2B(34): -4.8, 3B(10): 0.8	0.5
2016	BOS	MLB	21	20	39	-0.5	.571	0.3	3B(5): 0.2	0.0
2017	CHR	AAA	22	361	127	17.1	.379	-0.1	2B(80): 1.4	1.7
2017	CHA	MLB	22	231	92	4.2	.325	-0.7	2B(54): 5.8	1.0
2018	CHA	MLB	23	650	89	15.5	.344	-0.4	2B(149): -12.7	-0.2
2019	CHA	MLB	24	630	91	9.7	.318	0.5	3B 13, 2B -1	2.2

Yoan Moncada, continued

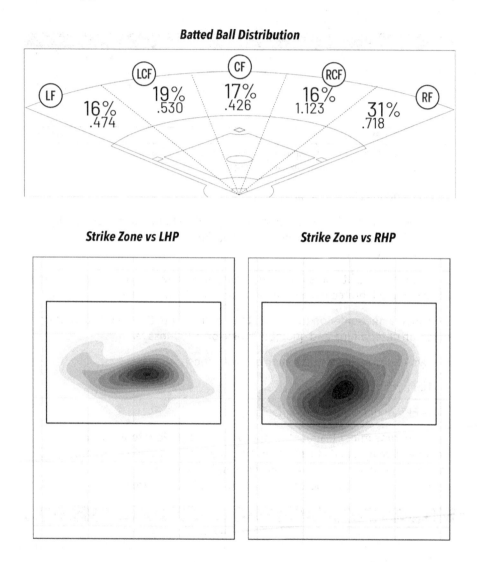

Batted Ball Distribution

Strike Zone vs LHP   **Strike Zone vs RHP**

Daniel Palka   OF

Born: 10/28/91   Age: 27   Bats: L   Throws: L
Height: 6'2"   Weight: 220   Origin: Round 3, 2013 Draft (#88 overall)

YEAR	TEAM	LVL	AGE	PA	R	2B	3B	HR	RBI	BB	K	SB	CS	AVG/OBP/SLG
2016	CHT	AA	24	345	42	12	4	21	65	38	100	7	4	.270/.348/.547
2016	ROC	AAA	24	223	31	12	0	13	25	18	86	2	1	.232/.296/.483
2017	ROC	AAA	25	362	47	13	3	11	42	27	80	1	2	.274/.329/.431
2018	CHR	AAA	26	73	11	3	0	3	7	10	21	1	2	.286/.384/.476
2018	CHA	MLB	26	449	56	15	3	27	67	30	153	2	1	.240/.294/.484
2019	CHA	MLB	27	448	50	16	2	19	58	33	144	2	1	.217/.278/.405

Breakout: 9%   Improve: 35%   Collapse: 11%   Attrition: 20%   MLB: 66%
Comparables: Casper Wells, Nelson Cruz, Carlos Peguero

Webster's defines Palkamania as:

—A specific sect of hedonism that values smoked home runs over equally valuable but less flashy concepts, such as outfield defense and taking the occasional pitch

—Recognition that home runs and rippling line drives are objectively fun and worth being celebrated even from fundamentally limited players

—A media phenomenon that is localized to the South Side of Chicago when there's an entertaining and quotable rookie on a 100-loss team

—Overexposure to intensely high exit velocities, and

—Not a real word

The BP Annual defines Palkamania as:

—A longtime minor leaguer thumper with one standout tool surprising everyone with his ability to actualize his double-plus raw power in games against major league pitching, even while defensive limitations and a hyper-aggressive approach perpetuate doubts about his long-term role

YEAR	TEAM	LVL	AGE	PA	DRC+	VORP	BABIP	BRR	FRAA	WARP
2016	CHT	AA	24	345	127	25.4	.324	-1.4	RF(66): -11.3, 1B(3): -0.5	-0.5
2016	ROC	AAA	24	223	111	5.9	.324	-2.3	RF(47): -4.9	-0.4
2017	ROC	AAA	25	362	104	10.0	.329	1.2	RF(61): 3.5, LF(25): 0.1	0.9
2018	CHR	AAA	26	73	123	3.7	.385	0.1	RF(15): 0.5	0.3
2018	CHA	MLB	26	449	100	11.8	.308	-0.8	RF(43): -3.0, LF(26): -0.5	0.4
2019	CHA	MLB	27	448	81	0.6	.284	-0.5	RF -5, LF -1	-0.6

Daniel Palka, continued

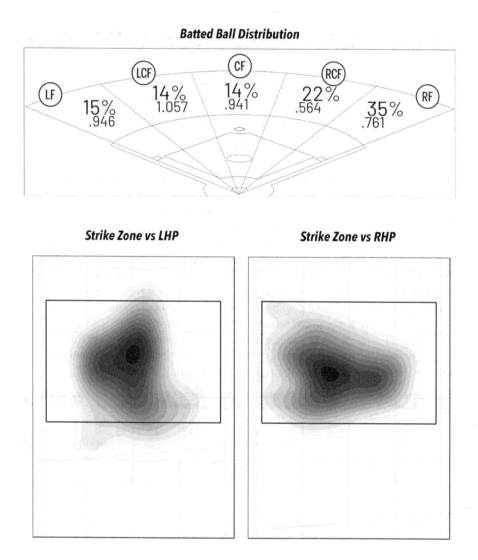

Batted Ball Distribution

LF 15% .946 · LCF 14% 1.057 · CF 14% .941 · RCF 22% .564 · 35% .761 RF

Strike Zone vs LHP

Strike Zone vs RHP

Yolmer Sanchez   INF

Born: 06/29/92   Age: 27   Bats: B   Throws: R
Height: 5'11"   Weight: 185   Origin: International Free Agent, 2009

YEAR	TEAM	LVL	AGE	PA	R	2B	3B	HR	RBI	BB	K	SB	CS	AVG/OBP/SLG
2016	CHR	AAA	24	260	31	11	2	8	29	17	55	10	4	.255/.309/.421
2016	CHA	MLB	24	163	15	9	1	4	21	5	42	0	1	.208/.236/.357
2017	CHA	MLB	25	534	63	19	8	12	59	35	111	8	9	.267/.319/.413
2018	CHA	MLB	26	662	62	34	10	8	55	49	138	14	6	.242/.306/.372
2019	CHA	MLB	27	579	68	25	6	12	52	41	124	10	6	.243/.304/.382

Breakout: 8%   Improve: 42%   Collapse: 12%   Attrition: 21%   MLB: 91%
Comparables: Cory Spangenberg, Lonnie Chisenhall, Andy LaRoche

Only a few weeks after they displaced him with second baseman of the future Yoan Moncada in July of 2017, the White Sox conceded that Sanchez's spunky combination of adept glovework, gap power and borderline hyperactive energy actually made him the most capable third baseman on their major league roster, even if everything about his game has always screamed "utilityman on a good team." Sanchez probably drew the most national attention to himself for dunking a Gatorade bucket over his own head during celebrations of the White Sox' few walk-off wins. He's an unflinchingly positive presence on a team willfully enduring dire straits, who effortlessly blends a new school focus on enjoying the moment with old school bromides of constant hustle and has made himself into an affable avatar of the franchise. And as a second half power outage proved, he's still a utilityman filling in at third base, so his staying power will always be moment-to-moment, even as he's living in said moment.

YEAR	TEAM	LVL	AGE	PA	DRC+	VORP	BABIP	BRR	FRAA	WARP
2016	CHR	AAA	24	260	88	1.8	.299	-1.5	2B(45): -0.5, SS(16): 1.8	0.1
2016	CHA	MLB	24	163	66	-4.9	.257	-1.2	2B(33): -1.8, 3B(6): 0.3	-0.5
2017	CHA	MLB	25	534	93	13.2	.321	0.9	2B(78): -0.3, 3B(52): 3.2	1.6
2018	CHA	MLB	26	662	80	11.8	.300	0.7	3B(141): -1.2, 2B(9): 0.2	0.7
2019	CHA	MLB	27	579	80	5.8	.289	0.1	2B -2, 3B 0	0.2

Yolmer Sanchez, continued

Batted Ball Distribution

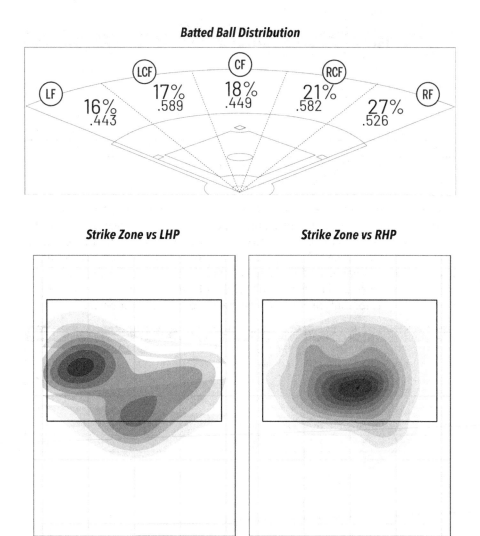

Strike Zone vs LHP

Strike Zone vs RHP

Preston Tucker   LF

Born: 07/06/90   Age: 28   Bats: L   Throws: L
Height: 6'0"   Weight: 210   Origin: Round 7, 2012 Draft (#219 overall)

YEAR	TEAM	LVL	AGE	PA	R	2B	3B	HR	RBI	BB	K	SB	CS	AVG/OBP/SLG
2016	FRE	AAA	25	229	35	14	3	8	29	15	49	1	1	.301/.349/.512
2016	HOU	MLB	25	144	11	8	1	4	8	8	40	0	0	.164/.222/.328
2017	FRE	AAA	26	569	84	20	7	24	96	65	102	2	3	.250/.333/.465
2018	GWN	AAA	27	62	7	4	1	0	6	2	5	0	0	.250/.274/.350
2018	CIN	MLB	27	42	4	1	0	2	5	4	9	0	0	.189/.286/.378
2018	ATL	MLB	27	142	15	10	0	4	22	9	34	0	0	.240/.303/.411
2019	CHA	MLB	28	251	26	10	2	9	32	20	58	0	0	.218/.284/.395

Breakout: 4%   Improve: 31%   Collapse: 15%   Attrition: 28%   MLB: 70%
Comparables: Ryan Rua, Xavier Paul, Jorge Piedra

Poor Tucker got thrown back and forth like a middle school dodgeball in P.E. class. He was dealt to Cincinnati in July as part of the Adam Duvall swap, only to be returned to Atlanta in September for cash. He actually didn't hit that badly in his Braves stints and gave them an outfield option they could confidently turn to in a pinch. He is what he is, though, further proof when he was outrighted on Halloween. Tucker is on track to be a useful outfield bench option for years to come, probably for multiple teams. May the yo-yo feeling commence.

YEAR	TEAM	LVL	AGE	PA	DRC+	VORP	BABIP	BRR	FRAA	WARP
2016	FRE	AAA	25	229	124	16.9	.355	0.5	RF(25): -4.0, LF(23): -0.3	0.3
2016	HOU	MLB	25	144	66	-6.0	.200	0.2	LF(19): -1.5, RF(3): -0.2	-0.5
2017	FRE	AAA	26	569	95	15.8	.263	-0.9	RF(54): -8.8, LF(35): 3.9	-0.4
2018	GWN	AAA	27	62	72	-0.6	.273	0.4	LF(14): 0.1	-0.1
2018	CIN	MLB	27	42	91	-0.1	.192	-0.2	LF(10): -2.6	-0.2
2018	ATL	MLB	27	142	86	4.6	.293	0.4	LF(27): 1.2, RF(4): -0.2	0.3
2019	CHA	MLB	28	251	87	3.3	.252	0.1	LF -1, RF 0	0.2

Preston Tucker, continued

Batted Ball Distribution

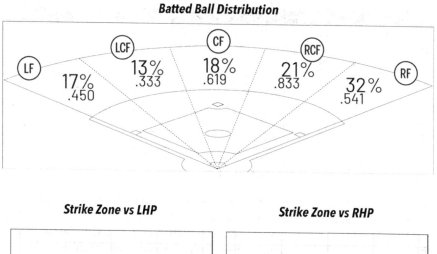

Strike Zone vs LHP   Strike Zone vs RHP

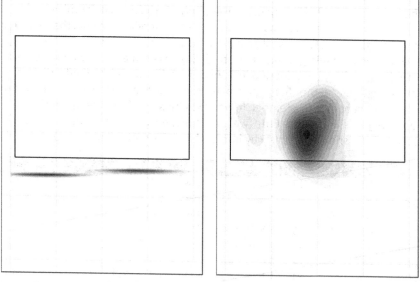

Ryan Burr RHP

Born: 05/28/94   Age: 25   Bats: R   Throws: R
Height: 6'4"   Weight: 225   Origin: Round 5, 2015 Draft (#136 overall)

YEAR	TEAM	LVL	AGE	W	L	SV	G	GS	IP	H	HR	BB/9	K/9	K	GB%	BABIP
2016	KNC	A	22	1	2	0	14	0	21	22	0	3.9	7.7	18	43%	.328
2017	KNC	A	23	1	2	4	22	0	32	29	3	4.2	12.9	46	48%	.361
2017	VIS	A+	23	1	0	1	17	0	25	13	0	2.2	10.4	29	74%	.245
2017	WNS	A+	23	0	0	1	6	0	8¹	5	0	5.4	14.0	13	47%	.333
2018	BIR	AA	24	4	2	2	30	0	43	30	3	4.8	9.0	43	51%	.248
2018	CHR	AAA	24	0	1	0	7	0	8¹	4	0	2.2	8.6	8	80%	.200
2018	CHA	MLB	24	0	0	0	8	0	9²	12	3	5.6	5.6	6	39%	.321
2019	CHA	MLB	25	2	2	0	41	0	43	41	6	5.4	8.9	42	45%	.296

Breakout: 4%   Improve: 8%   Collapse: 9%   Attrition: 14%   MLB: 18%
Comparables: Kevin McCarthy, Jose Ortega, Angel Nesbitt

Burr was already 20 years old when Lin-Manuel Miranda's *Hamilton* premiered at The Public Theater in New York City. He was into his third professional season when he was traded into the White Sox organization and placed at the same affiliate as fellow relief prospect Ian Hamilton. He did not ask for this life, and all the jokes and themed promos for the team social media accounts that are likely coming with it. He also was taken a bit by surprise by his call-up at the end of 2018, a season that began with him struggling to command his 95 mph four-seamer/hard slider combination in Double-A until June, and ended with him struggling to regain the "hard" part of his slider as he adjusted to the seams on major league balls in September. In between those months, and all the Hamilton jokes, was a nice little (well, not little, he's 6'4", 225 pounds) relief prospect who should find his way into sixth and seventh innings in 2019.

YEAR	TEAM	LVL	AGE	WHIP	ERA	DRA	WARP	MPH	FB%	WHF	CSP
2016	KNC	A	22	1.48	3.86	4.98	-0.1				
2017	KNC	A	23	1.38	2.81	3.17	0.7				
2017	VIS	A+	23	0.76	0.72	3.68	0.4				
2017	WNS	A+	23	1.20	0.00	5.20	0.0				
2018	BIR	AA	24	1.23	2.72	3.48	0.7				
2018	CHR	AAA	24	0.72	1.08	3.42	0.2				
2018	CHA	MLB	24	1.86	7.45	6.33	-0.2	96.1	67.5	11.5	52.4
2019	CHA	MLB	25	1.55	5.16	5.20	0.0	95.8	69.1	11.7	53.7

Ryan Burr, continued

Pitch Shape vs LHH   ## Pitch Shape vs RHH

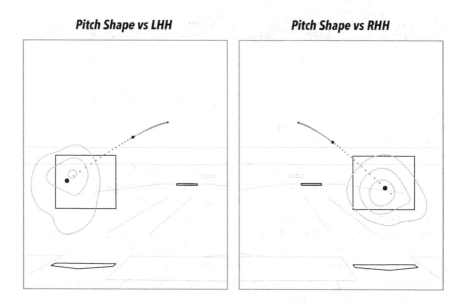

Type		Frequency	Velocity	H Movement	V Movement
●	Fastball	67.5%	95.3 [109]	-3.2 [116]	-12.9 [109]
□	Sinker				
+	Cutter	2.5%	90.2 [108]	4.2 [114]	-23.9 [99]
▲	Changeup	1.9%	85.5 [101]	-5.6 [130]	-21.7 [117]
✕	Splitter	5.7%	87.3 [109]	0 [131]	-26.1 [115]
▽	Slider	22.3%	83.4 [95]	2.9 [91]	-39.4 [81]
◇	Curveball				
⊕	Slow Curveball				
✳	Knuckleball				
▼	Screwball				

Alex Colome   RHP

Born: 12/31/88   Age: 30   Bats: R   Throws: R
Height: 6'1"   Weight: 220   Origin: International Free Agent, 2007

YEAR	TEAM	LVL	AGE	W	L	SV	G	GS	IP	H	HR	BB/9	K/9	K	GB%	BABIP
2016	TBA	MLB	27	2	4	37	57	0	56²	43	6	2.4	11.3	71	49%	.280
2017	TBA	MLB	28	2	3	47	65	0	66²	57	4	3.1	7.8	58	50%	.275
2018	TBA	MLB	29	2	5	11	23	0	21²	24	1	3.3	9.6	23	55%	.354
2018	SEA	MLB	29	5	0	1	47	0	46¹	35	6	2.5	9.5	49	42%	.254
2019	CHA	MLB	30	2	3	16	51	0	53	47	6	3.4	9.6	57	47%	.294

Breakout: 25%   Improve: 59%   Collapse: 26%   Attrition: 11%   MLB: 97%
Comparables: Blake Treinen, Chad Qualls, Phil Coke

It's not so much that the game passed the recently age-30 Colome by so much as its tastes did. The work of a perfectly solid, one-inning-per-game, one-run-every-three setup man was en vogue a few years ago, when everyone was trying to stock deep, well-rounded bullpens. But then we fell in love with copying Andrew Miller, and now it's 15 K/9 closers or bust. Colome performed perfectly well after coming over to Seattle to assist Edwin Diaz in a salary cutting trade, and then that same salary propelled him to the South Side, where he'll compete for save chances with Nate Jones. He'll either win that job, or lose it. And afterwards, he'll pitch just fine.

YEAR	TEAM	LVL	AGE	WHIP	ERA	DRA	WARP	MPH	FB%	WHF	CSP
2016	TBA	MLB	27	1.02	1.91	2.85	1.4	96.7	51.9	16.1	45.9
2017	TBA	MLB	28	1.20	3.24	3.97	0.9	95.9	32.7	12.4	46.8
2018	TBA	MLB	29	1.48	4.15	3.91	0.3	95.5	49.3	16	48.9
2018	SEA	MLB	29	1.04	2.53	3.97	0.5	96.5	49.3	15	45.5
2019	CHA	MLB	30	1.26	3.45	3.85	0.8	95.4	44.2	14.5	46.4

Alex Colome, continued

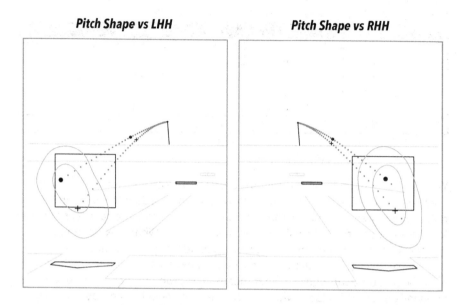

Pitch Shape vs LHH   ### Pitch Shape vs RHH

Type		Frequency	Velocity	H Movement	V Movement
●	Fastball	44.6%	95.6 [110]	-3.3 [116]	-11.5 [114]
□	Sinker	0.4%	96 [118]	-9.5 [126]	-13.7 [122]
+	Cutter	54.7%	91 [113]	1.7 [99]	-23.3 [102]
▲	Changeup	0.4%	90.7 [121]	-5.2 [132]	-20.5 [120]
✕	Splitter				
▽	Slider				
◇	Curveball				
⊕	Slow Curveball				
✳	Knuckleball				
▼	Screwball				

Dylan Covey   RHP

Born: 08/14/91   Age: 27   Bats: R   Throws: R
Height: 6'2"   Weight: 195   Origin: Round 4, 2013 Draft (#131 overall)

YEAR	TEAM	LVL	AGE	W	L	SV	G	GS	IP	H	HR	BB/9	K/9	K	GB%	BABIP
2016	MID	AA	24	2	1	0	6	6	29^1	21	2	5.2	8.0	26	61%	.247
2017	CHR	AAA	25	0	0	0	2	0	6	5	1	1.5	4.5	3	58%	.222
2017	CHA	MLB	25	0	7	0	18	12	70	83	20	4.4	5.3	41	49%	.296
2018	CHR	AAA	26	3	1	0	7	7	38^2	32	3	3.5	8.1	35	57%	.282
2018	CHA	MLB	26	5	14	0	27	21	121^2	129	13	3.8	6.7	91	56%	.302
2019	CHA	MLB	27	3	5	0	13	13	68	71	10	4.3	7.2	55	52%	.295

Breakout: 14%   Improve: 33%   Collapse: 16%   Attrition: 26%   MLB: 70%
Comparables: Williams Perez, Colin Rea, Shawn Hill

Year 2 of being pulled from the minors, dropped into a major league rotation only for a successive run of rough nights and harrowing days to route him to the bullpen went better for Covey than Year 1 of... more or less the same experience. Michael Kopech's torn UCL ushered him back into the White Sox rotation at year's end, and more importantly, he forged an identity on the mound as someone who is going to live and die with his sinker. The frequency of the dying after the first time through the order means he is probably well-advised to make his living out of the bullpen, where his two-seamer velocity can stay closer to the 95-96 mph band, but the state of the Sox rotation means a Year 3 could be in the works.

YEAR	TEAM	LVL	AGE	WHIP	ERA	DRA	WARP	MPH	FB%	WHF	CSP
2016	MID	AA	24	1.30	1.84	3.67	0.5				
2017	CHR	AAA	25	1.00	3.00	4.09	0.1				
2017	CHA	MLB	25	1.67	7.71	7.88	-1.9	94.6	60.5	6.8	45.5
2018	CHR	AAA	26	1.22	2.33	4.62	0.4				
2018	CHA	MLB	26	1.49	5.18	5.15	0.2	96.1	61.5	7.8	49.6
2019	CHA	MLB	27	1.51	4.91	5.30	0.1	95.1	62	7.6	48.4

Dylan Covey, continued

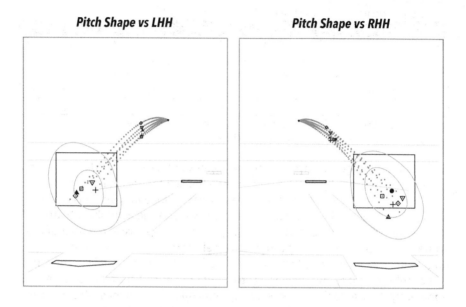

Type		Frequency	Velocity	H Movement	V Movement
●	Fastball	4.0%	94.7 [107]	-6.5 [101]	-14.8 [103]
☐	Sinker	57.5%	94.4 [110]	-11 [113]	-17.7 [109]
+	Cutter	5.0%	91.3 [115]	3 [107]	-21.2 [110]
▲	Changeup	11.6%	85.2 [99]	-7.9 [118]	-29.4 [94]
✕	Splitter				
▽	Slider	11.3%	87.6 [114]	4.3 [97]	-28.7 [113]
◇	Curveball	10.6%	81.7 [112]	3.2 [80]	-40.2 [118]
⊕	Slow Curveball				
✳	Knuckleball				
▼	Screwball				

Jace Fry LHP

Born: 07/09/93   Age: 25   Bats: L   Throws: L
Height: 6'1"   Weight: 190   Origin: Round 3, 2014 Draft (#77 overall)

YEAR	TEAM	LVL	AGE	W	L	SV	G	GS	IP	H	HR	BB/9	K/9	K	GB%	BABIP
2017	BIR	AA	23	2	1	3	33	0	45¹	36	1	4.8	10.3	52	59%	.307
2017	CHA	MLB	23	0	0	0	11	0	6²	12	1	6.8	4.1	3	39%	.407
2018	CHR	AAA	24	0	0	0	5	0	6²	3	1	0.0	14.9	11	54%	.167
2018	CHA	MLB	24	2	3	4	59	1	51¹	37	4	3.5	12.3	70	47%	.277
2019	CHA	MLB	25	2	2	4	46	0	48	39	5	4.3	11.3	61	48%	.296

Breakout: 36%   Improve: 56%   Collapse: 19%   Attrition: 20%   MLB: 85%
Comparables: Jensen Lewis, Cam Bedrosian, Jose Mijares

Fry's triumphant recovery from a second Tommy John surgery and subsequent reallocation to the bullpen were undercut by the fact that his major league debut went, well, quite poorly. So it threw everyone for a loop that his return from yet another disabled list stint to start 2018—this time a humble oblique strain—spurred his emergence as arguably the most impressive member of the White Sox bullpen. He doesn't throw extremely hard, nor does he wield a dominant wipeout offering to point to as the fuel to his short relief success, and was absolutely not an overpowering strikeout pitcher as a starter in college. Apparently the whole thing where a crafty lefty mixes five pitches, all of out the same slot, and throws them all for strikes with good deception can be really effective out of the bullpen. Whether that means every soft-tossing southpaw is a relief ace in waiting is more doubtful, but it's certainly turned Fry into a valuable asset.

YEAR	TEAM	LVL	AGE	WHIP	ERA	DRA	WARP	MPH	FB%	WHF	CSP
2017	BIR	AA	23	1.32	2.78	3.23	0.8				
2017	CHA	MLB	23	2.55	10.80	5.83	0.0	95.5	68.2	10.8	41.1
2018	CHR	AAA	24	0.45	1.35	2.02	0.2				
2018	CHA	MLB	24	1.11	4.38	2.96	1.2	95.2	34.2	15.3	43.7
2019	CHA	MLB	25	1.29	3.21	3.64	0.8	94.9	38.6	15.2	43.6

Jace Fry, continued

Pitch Shape vs LHH   Pitch Shape vs RHH

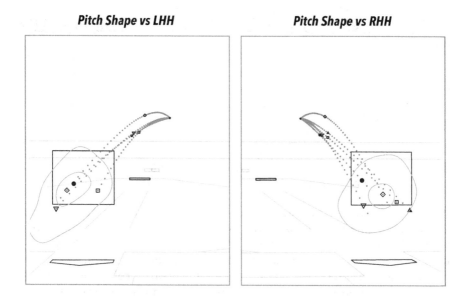

Type	Frequency	Velocity	H Movement	V Movement
● Fastball	15.1%	93.8 [104]	6.6 [100]	-14 [105]
☐ Sinker	19.1%	92.6 [101]	13.4 [93]	-22.9 [92]
+ Cutter				
▲ Changeup	10.4%	85 [99]	11.4 [99]	-29 [95]
✕ Splitter				
▽ Slider	31.8%	88.5 [118]	-0.9 [83]	-30.6 [107]
◇ Curveball	23.6%	77.2 [95]	-6.6 [95]	-52.9 [89]
⊕ Slow Curveball				
✳ Knuckleball				
▼ Screwball				

Carson Fulmer   RHP

Born: 12/13/93   Age: 25   Bats: R   Throws: R
Height: 6'0"   Weight: 195   Origin: Round 1, 2015 Draft (#8 overall)

YEAR	TEAM	LVL	AGE	W	L	SV	G	GS	IP	H	HR	BB/9	K/9	K	GB%	BABIP
2016	BIR	AA	22	4	9	0	17	17	87	82	7	5.3	9.3	90	45%	.310
2016	CHA	MLB	22	0	2	0	8	0	11²	12	2	5.4	7.7	10	44%	.312
2016	CHR	AAA	22	2	1	0	4	4	16	14	1	2.8	7.9	14	61%	.289
2017	CHR	AAA	23	7	9	0	25	25	126	132	18	4.6	6.9	96	46%	.297
2017	CHA	MLB	23	3	1	0	7	5	23¹	16	4	5.0	7.3	19	31%	.190
2018	CHA	MLB	24	2	4	0	9	8	32¹	37	8	6.7	8.1	29	34%	.296
2018	CHR	AAA	24	5	6	0	25	9	67²	70	10	5.5	8.2	62	40%	.316
2019	CHA	MLB	25	2	2	0	46	0	48	44	6	5.2	8.9	48	41%	.287

Breakout: 29%   Improve: 39%   Collapse: 12%   Attrition: 36%   MLB: 60%
Comparables: Zach Miner, Jose Cisnero, Josh Hall

Well, the White Sox certainly tried. There were plenty of evaluators who felt Carson Fulmer was bound to be a reliever even when he was a star at Vanderbilt, and the Sox took him eighth overall. Despite minor league numbers always riddled with control problems, numerous tweaks to slow down his herky-jerky motion that didn't quite take, and struggles to maintain his college velocity and stuff, Chicago rewarded every hint of progress with a shot at the big league rotation. That continued despite a rocky spring training in 2018, but their ambitions for him couldn't survive watching him get blitzed out of the game before the fifth every other start under the big league lights. Despite a pledge that he would return to the majors soon after being optioned in May, Fulmer never gave the Sox a reason to recall him, and after a few more trying months in Triple-A, they finally conceded that he's a reliever. The question for him going forward is whether he can show signs of a being a good one.

YEAR	TEAM	LVL	AGE	WHIP	ERA	DRA	WARP	MPH	FB%	WHF	CSP
2016	BIR	AA	22	1.53	4.76	3.49	1.7				
2016	CHA	MLB	22	1.63	8.49	3.76	0.2	95.3	50.2	10.4	40.5
2016	CHR	AAA	22	1.19	3.94	6.18	-0.2				
2017	CHR	AAA	23	1.56	5.79	5.11	0.8				
2017	CHA	MLB	23	1.24	3.86	7.31	-0.5	94.6	51.8	9.6	46.1
2018	CHA	MLB	24	1.89	8.07	8.06	-1.0	94.3	55.3	7.3	44.8
2018	CHR	AAA	24	1.64	5.32	4.97	0.3				
2019	CHA	MLB	25	1.48	4.92	5.04	0.1	94.2	54.9	8.6	45.3

Carson Fulmer, continued

Pitch Shape vs LHH   ## Pitch Shape vs RHH

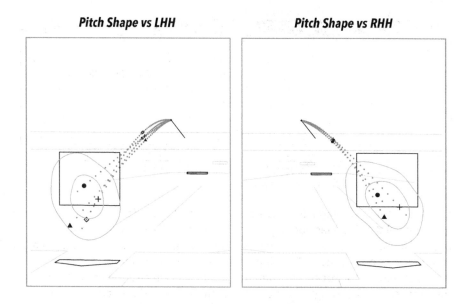

Type		Frequency	Velocity	H Movement	V Movement
●	Fastball	55.1%	93.5 [103]	-7.2 [98]	-13.8 [106]
□	Sinker	0.2%	94 [108]	-14.6 [83]	-15.8 [115]
+	Cutter	22.1%	89 [101]	4 [112]	-24 [99]
▲	Changeup	15.1%	86.7 [105]	-12.8 [92]	-27.6 [99]
✕	Splitter				
▽	Slider				
◇	Curveball	7.6%	81.6 [112]	8.6 [103]	-39.3 [120]
⊕	Slow Curveball				
✳	Knuckleball				
▼	Screwball				

Lucas Giolito   RHP

Born: 07/14/94   Age: 24   Bats: R   Throws: R
Height: 6'6"   Weight: 245   Origin: Round 1, 2012 Draft (#16 overall)

YEAR	TEAM	LVL	AGE	W	L	SV	G	GS	IP	H	HR	BB/9	K/9	K	GB%	BABIP
2016	HAR	AA	21	5	3	0	14	14	71	67	2	4.3	9.1	72	53%	.323
2016	HAG	A	21	0	0	0	1	1	7	6	2	0.0	5.1	4	36%	.200
2016	SYR	AAA	21	1	2	0	7	7	37¹	31	3	2.4	9.6	40	56%	.298
2016	WAS	MLB	21	0	1	0	6	4	21¹	26	7	5.1	4.6	11	42%	.271
2017	CHR	AAA	22	6	10	0	24	24	128²	122	17	4.1	9.4	134	45%	.312
2017	CHA	MLB	22	3	3	0	7	7	45¹	31	8	2.4	6.8	34	47%	.189
2018	CHA	MLB	23	10	13	0	32	32	173¹	166	27	4.7	6.5	125	45%	.268
2019	CHA	MLB	24	7	11	0	26	26	148	147	21	4.3	7.8	128	45%	.292

Breakout: 23%   Improve: 49%   Collapse: 15%   Attrition: 22%   MLB: 90%
Comparables: Martin Perez, Sean West, Sean Marshall

Giolito's 2018 was a search for a context other than "total disaster." For much of a grueling first half, it was about grinding without his best stuff, or without his best location, and competing even when unsteady mechanics robbed him of his command. As his second-half outings shaded more professional, his season drifted toward a story of growth, and the merits of letting a 24-year-old former top prospect work through his struggles, learn to make quicker adjustments and find the arm slot that allowed for the best balance between getting life on his fastball and actually putting it in the zone. Giolito's late-season success came from relying on his two-seamer, contradicting the carrying four-seamer and tumbling changeup approach that made him a success in spring training and the previous September. With how awful his 2018 season was in stretches, he just needed to show progress of any kind, which is why his disastrous close to the year was all the more discouraging. Starting in the majors requires consistency, and Giolito has still found preciously little.

YEAR	TEAM	LVL	AGE	WHIP	ERA	DRA	WARP	MPH	FB%	WHF	CSP
2016	HAR	AA	21	1.42	3.17	3.21	1.6				
2016	HAG	A	21	0.86	5.14	3.37	0.1				
2016	SYR	AAA	21	1.10	2.17	3.22	0.9				
2016	WAS	MLB	21	1.78	6.75	7.03	-0.4	96.1	71.1	6.3	48.1
2017	CHR	AAA	22	1.41	4.48	4.32	2.0				
2017	CHA	MLB	22	0.95	2.38	4.27	0.7	94.1	59.8	11.1	46.2
2018	CHA	MLB	23	1.48	6.13	6.58	-2.5	94.7	59.5	9.2	46.8
2019	CHA	MLB	24	1.47	4.86	5.25	0.3	94.5	62.1	9.6	48.4

Lucas Giolito, continued

Pitch Shape vs LHH   Pitch Shape vs RHH

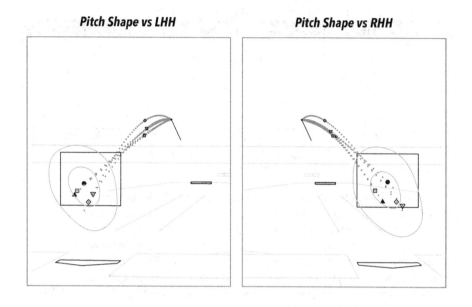

Type	Frequency	Velocity	H Movement	V Movement
● Fastball	39.5%	92.8 [101]	-6.7 [100]	-14.7 [103]
☐ Sinker	19.9%	92.8 [101]	-12.5 [101]	-18.3 [107]
+ Cutter				
▲ Changeup	15.3%	82.2 [88]	-9.1 [111]	-28.5 [97]
✕ Splitter				
▽ Slider	15.1%	84.2 [99]	3 [92]	-31.9 [103]
◇ Curveball	10.1%	79 [102]	8.1 [101]	-52 [91]
⊕ Slow Curveball				
✳ Knuckleball				
▼ Screwball				

Ian Hamilton   RHP

Born: 06/16/95   Age: 24   Bats: R   Throws: R
Height: 6'0"   Weight: 200   Origin: Round 11, 2016 Draft (#326 overall)

YEAR	TEAM	LVL	AGE	W	L	SV	G	GS	IP	H	HR	BB/9	K/9	K	GB%	BABIP
2016	KAN	A	21	1	1	8	21	0	31^2	22	3	4.0	7.7	27	49%	.235
2017	BIR	AA	22	1	3	1	14	0	19	26	0	3.8	10.4	22	52%	.419
2017	WNS	A+	22	3	3	6	30	0	52^2	33	1	1.4	8.9	52	46%	.241
2018	BIR	AA	23	2	1	12	21	0	25^1	20	0	4.3	12.1	34	47%	.323
2018	CHR	AAA	23	1	1	10	22	0	26^1	18	2	1.4	9.6	28	49%	.254
2018	CHA	MLB	23	1	2	0	10	0	8	6	2	2.2	5.6	5	48%	.174
2019	CHA	MLB	24	2	2	0	36	0	37^2	34	5	4.4	9.5	40	44%	.294

Breakout: 10%   Improve: 13%   Collapse: 8%   Attrition: 17%   MLB: 23%
Comparables: Heath Hembree, Abel De Los Santos, Diego Moreno

The short and unbelievably cut Ian Hamilton seems like he would be better suited leaking out of the backfield to catch screen passes, which would likely make better use of his plus speed than throwing off a mound. The thought definitely occurred to Hamilton, who was stopped from walking onto the Washington State football team only by the panicked efforts of a baseball coach anxious about seeing his closer getting laid out by 230-pound linebackers. Catching passes in the flat would be a waste of Hamilton's ability to sit 97-99 mph, a notable uptick from 2017, with command that sharpened over the course of the year. As he rapidly progressed from being a sorta-interesting reliever who threw sorta hard in High-A, to a completely dominant minor league closer, the scrutiny has heightened. With his short stature and arm action, Hamilton's fastball did not play as loud as its velocity in his big league debut, and he won't be able to survive stretches without feel for his slider like he did in Birmingham. But there's a real shot to carve out a big league relief future, where there was only a hint of one before.

YEAR	TEAM	LVL	AGE	WHIP	ERA	DRA	WARP	MPH	FB%	WHF	CSP
2016	KAN	A	21	1.14	3.69	3.04	0.6				
2017	BIR	AA	22	1.79	5.21	4.95	0.0				
2017	WNS	A+	22	0.78	1.71	2.82	1.3				
2018	BIR	AA	23	1.26	1.78	3.45	0.4				
2018	CHR	AAA	23	0.84	1.71	3.47	0.5				
2018	CHA	MLB	23	1.00	4.50	3.37	0.1	98.1	70.1	12	46.3
2019	CHA	MLB	24	1.40	4.39	4.62	0.2	97.9	72.2	12.3	47.7

Ian Hamilton, continued

Pitch Shape vs LHH	Pitch Shape vs RHH

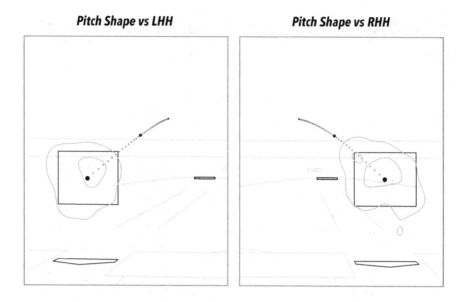

Type	Frequency	Velocity	H Movement	V Movement
● Fastball	70.1%	96.9 [114]	-7.1 [98]	-13.1 [108]
☐ Sinker				
+ Cutter				
▲ Changeup	6.0%	89.5 [117]	-10.7 [103]	-23.6 [111]
✕ Splitter				
▽ Slider	23.9%	89.2 [121]	1.3 [85]	-26.5 [119]
◇ Curveball				
⊕ Slow Curveball				
✳ Knuckleball				
▼ Screwball				

Kelvin Herrera   RHP

Born: 12/31/89   Age: 29   Bats: R   Throws: R
Height: 5'10"   Weight: 200   Origin: International Free Agent, 2006

YEAR	TEAM	LVL	AGE	W	L	SV	G	GS	IP	H	HR	BB/9	K/9	K	GB%	BABIP
2016	KCA	MLB	26	2	6	12	72	0	72	57	6	1.5	10.8	86	46%	.290
2017	KCA	MLB	27	3	3	26	64	0	59^1	60	9	3.0	8.5	56	47%	.295
2018	KCA	MLB	28	1	1	14	27	0	25^2	19	2	0.7	7.7	22	39%	.246
2018	WAS	MLB	28	1	2	3	21	0	18^2	24	4	3.9	7.7	16	36%	.333
2019	CHA	MLB	29	2	3	10	51	0	53	52	8	2.9	8.5	51	42%	.290

Breakout: 27%   Improve: 45%   Collapse: 31%   Attrition: 16%   MLB: 99%
Comparables: Sparky Lyle, Doug Corbett, Peter Moylan

When Herrera was traded to the D.C. in June, he had a 1.05 ERA and seemed to be sailing away from a turbulent 2017 spent thrashing against a long-ball attack. Little did he know, his homer monster was not vanquished, but merely lying in wait in the Anacostia River. He allowed five of his six dingers in just 18 2/3 innings with the Nationals before his season succumbed to a foot injury. Of course, monsters are usually manifestations of something internal. Maybe iffy command. Maybe pitch tipping? Whatever the specific demon, it stole his ability to convince hitters to chase. Usually accomplished with his changeup or slider, that key cog of his profile vanished in the months before he hit the free agent market.

YEAR	TEAM	LVL	AGE	WHIP	ERA	DRA	WARP	MPH	FB%	WHF	CSP
2016	KCA	MLB	26	0.96	2.75	2.39	2.1	99.7	60	16.2	47.3
2017	KCA	MLB	27	1.35	4.25	3.82	0.9	99.3	66.6	13.2	48.6
2018	KCA	MLB	28	0.82	1.05	3.88	0.3	98.5	64.9	15.7	48.3
2018	WAS	MLB	28	1.71	4.34	4.20	0.2	98.6	62.6	12.9	46.6
2019	CHA	MLB	29	1.29	4.44	4.67	0.3	98.5	63.7	14.5	47.8

Kelvin Herrera, continued

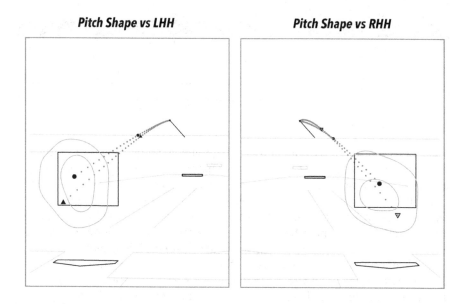

Type	Frequency	Velocity	H Movement	V Movement
● Fastball	63.8%	96.9 [114]	-8.3 [92]	-13.3 [108]
◻ Sinker				
+ Cutter				
▲ Changeup	17.2%	88.7 [114]	-11.6 [98]	-22.5 [114]
✕ Splitter				
▽ Slider	18.7%	81 [85]	14 [139]	-41.8 [74]
◇ Curveball	0.3%	80.1 [106]	12.2 [118]	-44.9 [107]
⊕ Slow Curveball				
✳ Knuckleball				
▼ Screwball				

Nate Jones   RHP

Born: 01/28/86   Age: 33   Bats: R   Throws: R
Height: 6'5"   Weight: 220   Origin: Round 5, 2007 Draft (#179 overall)

YEAR	TEAM	LVL	AGE	W	L	SV	G	GS	IP	H	HR	BB/9	K/9	K	GB%	BABIP
2016	CHA	MLB	30	5	3	3	3	0	70²	48	7	1.9	10.2	80	47%	.243
2017	CHA	MLB	31	1	0	0	11	0	11²	9	1	4.6	11.6	15	59%	.308
2018	CHA	MLB	32	2	2	5	33	0	30	28	4	4.5	9.6	32	41%	.289
2019	CHA	MLB	33	2	2	6	46	0	48	43	6	3.9	9.2	50	45%	.288

Breakout: 22%   Improve: 42%   Collapse: 29%   Attrition: 17%   MLB: 90%
Comparables: Jose Valverde, Jay Witasick, Kiko Calero

Nate Jones can still throw hard and miss bats when healthy. After missing three months in the middle of the 2018 with a pronator strain, sealing his fourth injury-marred season out of the last five, that was something he felt the need to work his way back and reaffirm, even at the end of a doomed campaign for a rebuilding team. Fastball-slider righties who can touch the upper-90s and strike out a batter per inning have become a lot more common since Jones first broke onto the scene in 2012, and he struggled with control problems that once seemed conquered in 2016 all while fighting off renewed elbow troubles. Still, there's a late-inning ceiling from a massive physical frame here, and as long as Jones continues to be willing to put the work in to get himself right, he'll get another chance to succeed.

YEAR	TEAM	LVL	AGE	WHIP	ERA	DRA	WARP	MPH	FB%	WHF	CSP
2016	CHA	MLB	30	0.89	2.29	2.84	1.7	99.2	63	15.3	48
2017	CHA	MLB	31	1.29	2.31	4.95	0.0	98.3	52.5	13	41.5
2018	CHA	MLB	32	1.43	3.00	4.55	0.1	98.6	64.7	15.2	47.1
2019	CHA	MLB	33	1.32	4.24	4.50	0.4	97.8	61.6	14.8	44.9

Nate Jones, continued

Pitch Shape vs LHH   ## Pitch Shape vs RHH

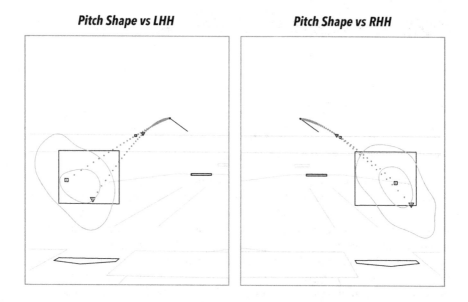

Type	Frequency	Velocity	H Movement	V Movement
● Fastball				
☐ Sinker	64.7%	97.7 [126]	-9.9 [123]	-12.1 [127]
+ Cutter				
▲ Changeup	2.1%	89.1 [115]	-10.3 [105]	-20.4 [121]
✕ Splitter				
▽ Slider	33.2%	89.3 [122]	2.5 [90]	-27.1 [118]
◇ Curveball				
⊕ Slow Curveball				
✳ Knuckleball				
▼ Screwball				

Michael Kopech RHP

Born: 04/30/96 Age: 23 Bats: R Throws: R
Height: 6'3" Weight: 205 Origin: Round 1, 2014 Draft (#33 overall)

YEAR	TEAM	LVL	AGE	W	L	SV	G	GS	IP	H	HR	BB/9	K/9	K	GB%	BABIP
2016	SLM	A+	20	4	1	0	11	11	52	25	1	5.0	14.2	82	45%	.273
2017	BIR	AA	21	8	7	0	22	22	119^1	77	6	4.5	11.7	155	42%	.272
2017	CHR	AAA	21	1	1	0	3	3	15	15	0	3.0	10.2	17	35%	.375
2018	CHR	AAA	22	7	7	0	24	24	126^1	101	9	4.3	12.1	170	40%	.316
2018	CHA	MLB	22	1	1	0	4	4	14^1	20	4	1.3	9.4	15	28%	.381
2019	CHA	MLB	23	6	8	0	24	24	118^2	97	13	5.0	11.4	151	39%	.297

Breakout: 20% Improve: 31% Collapse: 12% Attrition: 29% MLB: 51%
Comparables: Trevor May, Zack Wheeler, Tyler Thornburg

Every time a marquee pitching prospect goes down with a torn ulnar collateral ligament, the reaction resembles being diagnosed with a terminal illness. But after a season defined by Kopech overcoming his control problems, dealing with personal tragedy, and even gaining some consistency killing some changeups as he finally earned his way toward his major league debut, Tommy John surgery was a particularly undeserved denouement. Before he went down with injury, Kopech's social media feeds were notable for their documentation of his grueling training regimen. Before he threw in the triple-digits, from the age of six, he spent his days in Texas working out and throwing sunup to sundown in an empty pasture under his father's watchful eye. To what degree the fate of rehab from Tommy John surgery can be swayed by sheer work ethic, Kopech should earn high marks. But the rest is beyond him.

YEAR	TEAM	LVL	AGE	WHIP	ERA	DRA	WARP	MPH	FB%	WHF	CSP
2016	SLM	A+	20	1.04	2.25	2.78	1.6				
2017	BIR	AA	21	1.15	2.87	3.29	2.7				
2017	CHR	AAA	21	1.33	3.00	3.90	0.3				
2018	CHR	AAA	22	1.27	3.70	5.03	0.7				
2018	CHA	MLB	22	1.53	5.02	6.84	-0.3	97.7	62.5	10.9	50.9
2019	CHA	MLB	23	1.36	4.14	4.34	1.6	97.6	64.7	11.3	52.8

Michael Kopech, continued

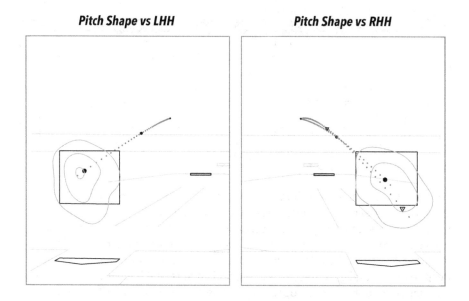

Type	Frequency	Velocity	H Movement	V Movement
● Fastball	62.5%	95.7 [110]	-8.8 [90]	-11.7 [113]
☐ Sinker				
＋ Cutter				
▲ Changeup	9.8%	88.9 [114]	-11.3 [100]	-25.1 [107]
✕ Splitter				
▽ Slider	27.7%	81.1 [85]	7.5 [111]	-38.9 [83]
◇ Curveball				
⊕ Slow Curveball				
✳ Knuckleball				
▼ Screwball				

Reynaldo Lopez   RHP

Born: 01/04/94   Age: 25   Bats: R   Throws: R
Height: 6'1"   Weight: 200   Origin: International Free Agent, 2012

YEAR	TEAM	LVL	AGE	W	L	SV	G	GS	IP	H	HR	BB/9	K/9	K	GB%	BABIP
2016	HAR	AA	22	3	5	0	14	14	76¹	69	7	2.9	11.8	100	43%	.320
2016	SYR	AAA	22	2	2	0	5	5	33	21	6	2.7	7.1	26	33%	.174
2016	WAS	MLB	22	5	3	0	11	6	44	47	4	4.5	8.6	42	43%	.326
2017	CHR	AAA	23	6	7	0	22	22	121	101	16	3.6	9.7	131	38%	.270
2017	CHA	MLB	23	3	3	0	8	8	47²	49	7	2.6	5.7	30	30%	.271
2018	CHA	MLB	24	7	10	0	32	32	188²	165	25	3.6	7.2	151	34%	.260
2019	CHA	MLB	25	7	11	0	26	26	148	147	26	3.7	8.3	136	37%	.287

Breakout: 14%   Improve: 53%   Collapse: 21%   Attrition: 24%   MLB: 95%
Comparables: Kendall Graveman, Travis Wood, David Huff

With the way Lopez's upper body leans back and then lurches forward in his three-quarters sling of a delivery, it would be wrong to say he comes by his top of the scale velocity easily, but it's certainly natural. And with the way he went from not throwing a slider at all in games in 2017 to leaning on it as a legit big league swing-and-miss offering in a year's time, he certainly is teachable. But despite the natural gifts, despite a curve and change that have also showed eye-opening potential at times, Lopez's overall performance remains less than the sum of its very intriguing parts, even as he grew better at avoiding the control lapses that marred his first half. Lopez edged closer to a future as a mid-to-back-end starter while many of his Sox teammates backflipped away from it, so he counts as a success story who earned the chance to continue progressing.

YEAR	TEAM	LVL	AGE	WHIP	ERA	DRA	WARP	MPH	FB%	WHF	CSP
2016	HAR	AA	22	1.23	3.18	2.32	2.5				
2016	SYR	AAA	22	0.94	3.27	4.87	0.2				
2016	WAS	MLB	22	1.57	4.91	4.86	0.2	98.7	64.3	10.4	47.8
2017	CHR	AAA	23	1.24	3.79	6.83	-1.5				
2017	CHA	MLB	23	1.32	4.72	6.40	-0.4	97.6	60.9	9	48.8
2018	CHA	MLB	24	1.27	3.91	5.65	-0.7	97.9	60.9	10	49.2
2019	CHA	MLB	25	1.38	4.96	5.36	0.1	97.6	62.7	10.1	49.9

Reynaldo Lopez, continued

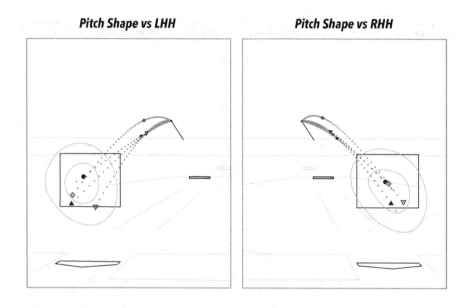

Type		Frequency	Velocity	H Movement	V Movement
●	Fastball	60.5%	95.9 [111]	-8.1 [93]	-13.6 [107]
☐	Sinker	0.4%	94.4 [109]	-10.7 [115]	-17.9 [108]
+	Cutter	1.3%	86.3 [85]	4.7 [116]	-28 [83]
▲	Changeup	15.5%	84 [94]	-10 [107]	-26.4 [103]
✕	Splitter				
▽	Slider	16.7%	84.1 [98]	3.7 [95]	-31.8 [103]
◇	Curveball	5.5%	76.1 [91]	4.3 [85]	-46.3 [104]
⊕	Slow Curveball				
✳	Knuckleball				
▼	Screwball				

Juan Minaya   RHP

Born: 09/18/90   Age: 28   Bats: R   Throws: R
Height: 6'4"   Weight: 210   Origin: International Free Agent, 2008

YEAR	TEAM	LVL	AGE	W	L	SV	G	GS	IP	H	HR	BB/9	K/9	K	GB%	BABIP
2016	FRE	AAA	25	1	3	0	17	0	25^1	25	1	3.6	6.8	19	51%	.308
2016	CHR	AAA	25	4	3	1	17	0	26^2	23	2	3.4	9.4	28	48%	.288
2016	CHA	MLB	25	1	0	0	11	0	10^1	10	0	4.4	5.2	6	24%	.294
2017	CHR	AAA	26	1	0	0	13	0	19	17	0	2.4	7.1	15	45%	.293
2017	CHA	MLB	26	3	2	9	40	0	43^2	38	7	4.1	10.5	51	34%	.304
2018	CHR	AAA	27	1	3	2	19	0	23^1	18	4	3.1	10.4	27	44%	.264
2018	CHA	MLB	27	2	2	1	52	0	46^2	39	3	5.6	11.2	58	43%	.310
2019	CHA	MLB	28	1	1	0	25	0	26	25	3	4.4	9.7	29	42%	.297

Breakout: 14%   Improve: 28%   Collapse: 22%   Attrition: 22%   MLB: 64%
Comparables: Clay Zavada, Brandon Cunniff, Jose Ramirez

When Minaya staggered off the mound in disgust on April 7, it was fair to wonder how many more times he would be seen on a major league field again. He was offered up for a lopsided ninth inning and for a team unlikely to play a high-leverage game all year, and walked four hitters in a row. Before his manager sat down for his postgame media briefing, Minaya was optioned to boot. As a live-armed, walk-addled waiver claim clutching at a spot in a rebuilding bullpen, he will likely always be one step back in command from career-threatening peril. But by mid-June he was back in the majors and attacking the strike zone with a lively mid-90s fastball and slider combination, and by the end of the year, it was debatable whether the Sox had a more reliable right-handed reliever. That's not ideal, as his control will always give his high-leverage work a flair for the dramatic, but it's major league quality stuff from a major league body, which is a decent start.

YEAR	TEAM	LVL	AGE	WHIP	ERA	DRA	WARP	MPH	FB%	WHF	CSP
2016	FRE	AAA	25	1.38	3.91	3.53	0.4				
2016	CHR	AAA	25	1.24	3.38	3.51	0.4				
2016	CHA	MLB	25	1.45	4.35	6.15	-0.1	96.6	65.6	10.6	46.9
2017	CHR	AAA	26	1.16	1.42	5.22	0.0				
2017	CHA	MLB	26	1.33	4.53	5.52	-0.2	95.7	62.8	12.5	46.9
2018	CHR	AAA	27	1.11	4.24	3.98	0.3				
2018	CHA	MLB	27	1.46	3.28	5.05	-0.1	96.5	61.2	12.4	45.2
2019	CHA	MLB	28	1.40	4.18	4.46	0.2	95.6	62.5	12.4	46.5

Juan Minaya, continued

Pitch Shape vs LHH   ### Pitch Shape vs RHH

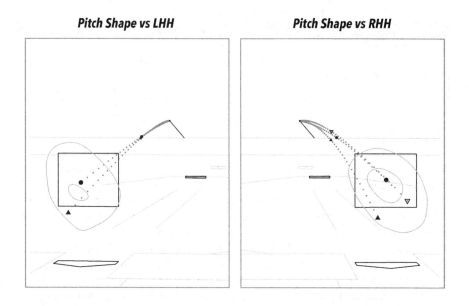

Type	Frequency	Velocity	H Movement	V Movement
● Fastball	61.2%	95.4 [109]	-8.6 [91]	-13.6 [107]
☐ Sinker				
+ Cutter				
▲ Changeup	23.1%	90.1 [119]	-11.2 [100]	-29.2 [94]
✕ Splitter				
▽ Slider	15.6%	86.3 [108]	4 [96]	-31.7 [104]
◇ Curveball				
⊕ Slow Curveball				
✳ Knuckleball				
▼ Screwball				

Ivan Nova   RHP

Born: 01/12/87   Age: 32   Bats: R   Throws: R
Height: 6'5"   Weight: 250   Origin: International Free Agent, 2004

YEAR	TEAM	LVL	AGE	W	L	SV	G	GS	IP	H	HR	BB/9	K/9	K	GB%	BABIP
2016	NYA	MLB	29	7	6	1	21	15	97¹	107	19	2.3	6.9	75	56%	.297
2016	PIT	MLB	29	5	2	0	11	11	64²	68	4	0.4	7.2	52	55%	.318
2017	PIT	MLB	30	11	14	0	31	31	187	203	29	1.7	6.3	131	48%	.299
2018	PIT	MLB	31	9	9	0	29	29	161	171	26	2.0	6.4	114	47%	.288
2019	CHA	MLB	32	8	10	0	26	26	148	162	24	2.4	6.8	112	48%	.299

Breakout: 24%   Improve: 50%   Collapse: 20%   Attrition: 15%   MLB: 88%
Comparables: Odalis Perez, Joe Blanton, Jon Lieber

After he was acquired from the Yankees in the middle of 2016, Nova was quickly touted as Yet Another Ray Searage Success Story™ after 64.2 glittering innings at the tail end of that campaign. Since then, Nova has been…adequate. Detractors might look at Nova's WARP the last three seasons and shrug, but there's nothing wrong with an arm that can churn out a 1-2 WARP season like clockwork. Every staff needs guys like this, particularly when they can reliably eat 160-plus innings per season. Nova continues to be decent against righties but miserable against left-handers, and even his splits the last three seasons have been eerily similar. Nova is like a plain bagel with cream cheese. It hits the spot and keeps your stomach full all morning but isn't a meal you're going to remember when lunch rolls around.

YEAR	TEAM	LVL	AGE	WHIP	ERA	DRA	WARP	MPH	FB%	WHF	CSP
2016	NYA	MLB	29	1.36	4.90	4.78	0.6	95.4	66.6	10.1	44.8
2016	PIT	MLB	29	1.10	3.06	3.68	1.2	95.6	62.1	10.2	50.7
2017	PIT	MLB	30	1.28	4.14	4.71	1.8	94.7	68.1	9	49.5
2018	PIT	MLB	31	1.28	4.19	4.60	1.3	94.8	66.9	9.7	46.6
2019	CHA	MLB	32	1.37	4.59	4.97	0.8	94.0	66.3	9.5	47.2

Ivan Nova, continued

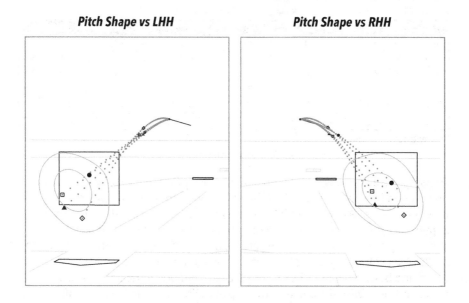

Pitch Shape vs LHH   **Pitch Shape vs RHH**

Type	Frequency	Velocity	H Movement	V Movement
● Fastball	31.9%	93.6 [103]	-11.3 [78]	-16.7 [97]
☐ Sinker	35.0%	93.2 [104]	-15.1 [80]	-22.1 [94]
+ Cutter				
▲ Changeup	12.0%	87 [107]	-14.2 [85]	-26.6 [102]
✕ Splitter				
▽ Slider				
◇ Curveball	21.1%	81 [109]	3.2 [80]	-42.9 [112]
⊕ Slow Curveball				
✳ Knuckleball				
▼ Screwball				

Carlos Rodon   LHP

Born: 12/10/92   Age: 26   Bats: L   Throws: L
Height: 6'3"   Weight: 235   Origin: Round 1, 2014 Draft (#3 overall)

YEAR	TEAM	LVL	AGE	W	L	SV	G	GS	IP	H	HR	BB/9	K/9	K	GB%	BABIP
2016	CHA	MLB	23	9	10	0	28	28	165	176	23	2.9	9.2	168	44%	.330
2017	CHR	AAA	24	0	3	0	3	3	13²	17	0	4.6	7.2	11	50%	.354
2017	CHA	MLB	24	2	5	0	12	12	69¹	64	12	4.0	9.9	76	45%	.297
2018	CHR	AAA	25	1	0	0	3	3	12²	10	0	3.6	15.6	22	56%	.435
2018	CHA	MLB	25	6	8	0	20	20	120²	97	15	4.1	6.7	90	42%	.243
2019	CHA	MLB	26	8	10	0	26	26	156	152	21	3.7	8.6	149	43%	.298

Breakout: 16%   Improve: 52%   Collapse: 15%   Attrition: 11%   MLB: 99%
Comparables: Johnny Cueto, John Danks, Vinegar Bend Mizell

To paraphrase one longtime baseball man, Carlos Rodon's 2018 season was pretty good for someone who had their throwing shoulder cut open the previous season. When his peripheral-defying dominance ran dry all at once in September, the encouraging suffix of "and he's doing this without all his best stuff" morphed into "wait until he gets his best stuff back." Rodon spent a lot of his 2018 season sitting in the low-90s and struggling to prove to hitters he could command both versions of his slider—the wipeout destroyer and the early count strike-grabber—with the old level of snap and bite. He ended his year, after a disastrous outing that saw him yanked before the end of the second inning in Minnesota, very optimistic that the next step in his recovery would be on display in 2019. His experience of being a high-contact pitcher would indicate that he'll need it.

YEAR	TEAM	LVL	AGE	WHIP	ERA	DRA	WARP	MPH	FB%	WHF	CSP
2016	CHA	MLB	23	1.39	4.04	4.81	1.0	97.5	63.3	10.9	48.3
2017	CHR	AAA	24	1.76	9.22	5.35	0.1				
2017	CHA	MLB	24	1.37	4.15	5.13	0.3	96.4	61.2	11.1	47.9
2018	CHR	AAA	25	1.18	1.42	3.00	0.4				
2018	CHA	MLB	25	1.26	4.18	6.57	-1.8	95.8	59.8	9.7	47.6
2019	CHA	MLB	26	1.39	4.37	4.73	1.3	96.1	62.5	10.6	48.7

Carlos Rodon, continued

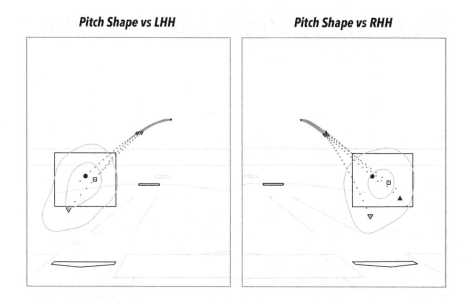

Pitch Shape vs LHH　　　**Pitch Shape vs RHH**

Type	Frequency	Velocity	H Movement	V Movement
● Fastball	49.2%	93.1 [102]	6.8 [99]	-14.9 [103]
☐ Sinker	10.6%	93.6 [106]	12.9 [97]	-18.2 [107]
+ Cutter				
▲ Changeup	14.0%	85.3 [100]	14.2 [85]	-28.9 [95]
✕ Splitter				
▽ Slider	26.1%	85.5 [105]	-5.9 [104]	-33.8 [98]
◇ Curveball				
⊕ Slow Curveball				
✳ Knuckleball				
▼ Screwball				

Ervin Santana   RHP

Born: 12/12/82   Age: 36   Bats: R   Throws: R
Height: 6'2"   Weight: 175   Origin: International Free Agent, 2000

YEAR	TEAM	LVL	AGE	W	L	SV	G	GS	IP	H	HR	BB/9	K/9	K	GB%	BABIP
2016	MIN	MLB	33	7	11	0	30	30	181¹	168	19	2.6	7.4	149	44%	.285
2017	MIN	MLB	34	16	8	0	33	33	211¹	177	31	2.6	7.1	167	43%	.245
2018	FTM	A+	35	0	2	0	3	3	10¹	7	1	0.9	6.1	7	32%	.200
2018	ROC	AAA	35	0	1	0	2	2	11²	6	3	3.1	6.2	8	31%	.103
2018	MIN	MLB	35	0	1	0	5	5	24²	31	9	3.3	5.8	16	23%	.282
2019	CHA	MLB	36	4	7	0	16	16	91	97	17	3.2	6.7	68	39%	.289

Breakout: 10%   Improve: 40%   Collapse: 21%   Attrition: 10%   MLB: 81%
Comparables: Warren Spahn, Phil Niekro, Early Wynn

Santana proved ageless for about as long as a pitcher can do so. From 2009 through 2017, he threw 93 mph, leaned heavily on a slider that missed bats with the best of them and racked up as many innings as his managers were willing to give him. For all those years, he showed no sign of wearing down. Like most pitchers who never wear down, however, Santana eventually broke. Offseason finger surgery didn't wholly mend him, and even in his brief time with the big-league team, he was nowhere near himself. His fastball velocity tumbled by four miles per hour, forcing him to make more use of his changeup and sinker. His slider stopped missing bats. At 36, even perfect health might not bring back the electricity his arm has lost.

YEAR	TEAM	LVL	AGE	WHIP	ERA	DRA	WARP	MPH	FB%	WHF	CSP
2016	MIN	MLB	33	1.22	3.38	4.05	2.7	95.6	52.6	10.7	43.7
2017	MIN	MLB	34	1.13	3.28	4.06	3.6	95.0	52.7	11.3	44.3
2018	FTM	A+	35	0.77	3.48	4.05	0.2				
2018	ROC	AAA	35	0.86	3.09	6.90	-0.2				
2018	MIN	MLB	35	1.62	8.03	8.84	-1.0	90.9	50.7	4.9	45.9
2019	CHA	MLB	36	1.41	5.29	5.73	-0.3	93.6	51.4	10.3	43.9

Ervin Santana, continued

Pitch Shape vs LHH

Pitch Shape vs RHH

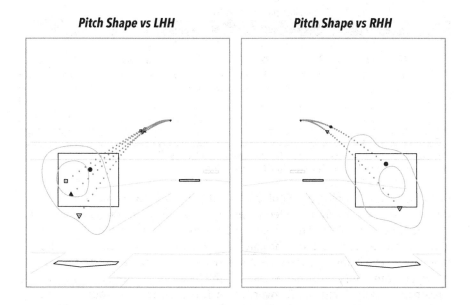

Type		Frequency	Velocity	H Movement	V Movement
●	Fastball	36.0%	89.3 [90]	-3.6 [114]	-18.4 [92]
□	Sinker	14.7%	88.3 [79]	-8.3 [136]	-20.1 [101]
+	Cutter				
▲	Changeup	18.5%	82.7 [90]	-7.4 [121]	-23.2 [112]
✕	Splitter				
▽	Slider	30.8%	81.4 [86]	4.8 [100]	-33.6 [98]
◇	Curveball				
⊕	Slow Curveball				
✳	Knuckleball				
▼	Screwball				

Thyago Vieira RHP

Born: 07/01/93   Age: 25   Bats: R   Throws: R
Height: 6'2"   Weight: 210   Origin: International Free Agent, 2010

YEAR	TEAM	LVL	AGE	W	L	SV	G	GS	IP	H	HR	BB/9	K/9	K	GB%	BABIP
2016	BAK	A+	22	1	0	0	8	34	0	44¹	37	1	3.7	10.8	53	53%	.313
2017	ARK	AA	23	2	3	2	29	0	36¹	30	1	3.7	8.7	35	49%	.293
2017	SEA	MLB	23	0	0	0	1	0	1	0	0	0.0	9.0	1	50%	.000
2017	TAC	AAA	23	0	1	2	12	0	17²	18	1	3.6	5.6	11	53%	.298
2018	CHR	AAA	24	0	4	6	36	0	41	40	2	5.3	11.0	50	43%	.349
2018	CHA	MLB	24	1	1	1	16	0	17²	21	4	4.6	7.6	15	33%	.315
2019	CHA	MLB	25	1	1	0	20	0	21	21	3	4.8	9.4	23	44%	.299

Breakout: 10%   Improve: 14%   Collapse: 6%   Attrition: 14%   MLB: 22%
Comparables: Brian Ellington, Craig Breslow, Angel Nesbitt

Pitching the ninth inning of a Sept. 8 blowout home loss to Anaheim, Vieira's third wild pitch of the frame sailed so far high and wide of his target and struck the backstop so firmly and true, that it rebounded perfectly into the waiting glove of catcher Kevan Smith. The catcher merely pivoted in place behind home plate to retrieve it, laying a tag on a stunned and then resigned Kaleb Cowart trying to score from third. That would do pretty well as a summary of Vieira's season in a nutshell, but an ERA over 5.00 at Triple-A Charlotte would also do well to show how Vieira's raw tools and prospect reputation outstripped his effectiveness as a reliever. It's very long road between being able to hit 100 on the gun and delivering clean innings on a consistent basis, and it's paved with a lot more strikes than Vieira threw in 2018.

YEAR	TEAM	LVL	AGE	WHIP	ERA	DRA	WARP	MPH	FB%	WHF	CSP
2016	BAK	A+	22	1.24	2.84	3.27	0.9				
2017	ARK	AA	23	1.24	3.72	3.42	0.6				
2017	SEA	MLB	23	0.00	0.00	4.46	0.0	100.7	70	0	42.4
2017	TAC	AAA	23	1.42	4.58	3.84	0.3				
2018	CHR	AAA	24	1.56	5.05	4.00	0.5				
2018	CHA	MLB	24	1.70	7.13	7.59	-0.5	99.0	80.3	11	50.6
2019	CHA	MLB	25	1.49	4.82	4.96	0.0	98.8	81.9	11	48.1

Thyago Vieira, continued

Pitch Shape vs LHH   ### Pitch Shape vs RHH

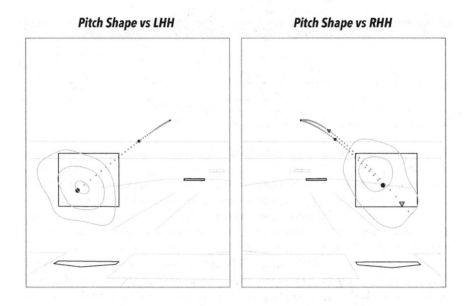

Type		Frequency	Velocity	H Movement	V Movement
●	Fastball	80.3%	96.8 [114]	-8.4 [92]	-12.4 [111]
□	Sinker				
+	Cutter				
▲	Changeup	3.4%	91 [123]	-11.9 [96]	-20.8 [119]
✕	Splitter				
▽	Slider	16.3%	84.4 [100]	5.7 [104]	-32.9 [100]
◇	Curveball				
⊕	Slow Curveball				
✳	Knuckleball				
▼	Screwball				

Micker Adolfo OF

Born: 09/11/96   Age: 22   Bats: R   Throws: R
Height: 6'3"   Weight: 200   Origin: International Free Agent, 2013

YEAR	TEAM	LVL	AGE	PA	R	2B	3B	HR	RBI	BB	K	SB	CS	AVG/OBP/SLG
2016	KAN	A	19	265	30	13	1	5	21	14	88	0	1	.219/.269/.340
2017	KAN	A	20	473	60	28	2	16	68	31	149	2	0	.264/.331/.453
2018	WNS	A+	21	336	48	18	1	11	50	34	92	2	1	.282/.369/.464
2019	CHA	MLB	22	251	22	8	0	9	28	10	92	0	0	.175/.220/.319

Breakout: 2%   Improve: 9%   Collapse: 0%   Attrition: 7%   MLB: 10%
Comparables: Chris Parmelee, Ryan O'Hearn, Lars Anderson

Watching Adolfo take batting practice with his best buddy Eloy Jimenez, it takes a studious eye to tell which one is the elite power-hitting prospect on the cusp of the major leagues, and which one is merely the prospect with elite raw power. The grind of annual injury (this year he was able to sneak in nearly 80 games of action between spraining his UCL in spring training and Tommy John surgery in July) has not prevented Adolfo in the least from adding muscle and strength. Against all odds, it has also not stalled the gradual progression of his once raw hitting approach, or the slow paring of his once-garish strikeout rate even as he advances through the lower minors. The real test of his approach and whether it holds up when he has to protect against top-level velocity is still on the way, and it will be years before he can hope to join Jimenez in Chicago, but he has exceeded expectations before.

YEAR	TEAM	LVL	AGE	PA	DRC+	VORP	BABIP	BRR	FRAA	WARP
2016	KAN	A	19	265	69	0.7	.318	0.0	RF(61): 8.9, CF(2): -0.2	0.1
2017	KAN	A	20	473	116	17.5	.366	-4.1	RF(102): -12.1	-0.8
2018	WNS	A+	21	336	137	14.6	.372	-1.5		0.8
2019	CHA	MLB	22	251	43	-14.2	.240	-0.5		-1.5

Luis Alexander Basabe CF

Born: 08/26/96   Age: 22   Bats: B   Throws: R
Height: 6'0"   Weight: 160   Origin: International Free Agent, 2012

YEAR	TEAM	LVL	AGE	PA	R	2B	3B	HR	RBI	BB	K	SB	CS	AVG/OBP/SLG
2016	GRN	A	19	451	61	24	8	12	52	40	116	25	5	.258/.325/.447
2017	WNS	A+	20	435	52	12	5	5	36	49	104	17	6	.221/.320/.320
2018	WNS	A+	21	245	36	12	5	9	30	34	64	7	8	.266/.370/.502
2018	BIR	AA	21	270	41	9	3	6	26	30	76	9	4	.251/.340/.394
2019	CHA	MLB	22	251	28	7	2	7	22	18	78	5	2	.179/.241/.312

Breakout: 6%   Improve: 26%   Collapse: 0%   Attrition: 14%   MLB: 31%
Comparables: Austin Jackson, Michael Saunders, Ryan Kalish

At this stage of his career, Hunter Greene seems pretty darn predictable in his pitch mix and arm action, and he finished his 2018 season a full two levels below where Basabe ended up. Still, when it comes to announcing your legitimacy to the world, turning one of Greene's 102 mph fastballs on the outer half into a massive opposite-field home run serves pretty well. A surgically-repaired left knee allowed Basabe to drive off the leg and tap into his not insubstantial raw power, complementing a speedy center fielder profile. There was an understandable learning curve for him to deal with upon his midseason promotion, but he held his own despite not turning 22 until the end of August. With the swing-and-miss present, there's still plenty of room for Basabe to stumble down the fourth outfielder path, but he's already shown pretty clear evidence that he's willing to adjust. When he was on deck, and 102 mph flashed on the radar gun, Basabe's Futures Game manager David Ortiz popped his head out of the dugout and barked at him to shorten up his swing. Basabe complied.

YEAR	TEAM	LVL	AGE	PA	DRC+	VORP	BABIP	BRR	FRAA	WARP
2016	GRN	A	19	451	113	26.3	.330	2.7	CF(98): 11.6	2.6
2017	WNS	A+	20	435	86	10.3	.292	4.4	CF(92): 0.1, RF(12): -0.4	0.2
2018	WNS	A+	21	245	141	19.7	.341	-2.0	CF(28): 2.2, LF(16): 1.5	1.4
2018	BIR	AA	21	270	106	13.3	.344	2.1	CF(42): -1.9, RF(15): 0.3	0.5
2019	CHA	MLB	22	251	51	-6.0	.231	0.3	CF 2, LF 0	-0.4

Zack Collins C

Born: 02/06/95   Age: 24   Bats: L   Throws: R
Height: 6'3"   Weight: 220   Origin: Round 1, 2016 Draft (#10 overall)

YEAR	TEAM	LVL	AGE	PA	R	2B	3B	HR	RBI	BB	K	SB	CS	AVG/OBP/SLG
2016	WNS	A+	21	153	24	7	0	6	18	33	39	0	0	.258/.418/.467
2017	WNS	A+	22	426	63	18	3	17	48	76	118	0	2	.223/.365/.443
2017	BIR	AA	22	45	7	2	0	2	5	11	11	0	0	.235/.422/.471
2018	BIR	AA	23	531	58	24	1	15	68	101	158	5	0	.234/.382/.404
2019	CHA	MLB	24	29	3	1	0	1	3	4	10	0	0	.167/.286/.333

Breakout: 10%   Improve: 14%   Collapse: 2%   Attrition: 17%   MLB: 34%
Comparables: Carlos Santana, Derek Norris, Travis Shaw

If Collins showed up around 10 years ago, this book might be touting him as a future star. He's a catcher who hits for decent power and walks more than literally any other player at his minor league level. But since this book costs

YEAR	TEAM	P. COUNT	FRM RUNS	BLK RUNS	THRW RUNS	TOT RUNS
2017	BIR	1559	-1.8	-0.3	0.0	-2.5
2018	BIR	10814	-12.2	-0.9	-0.7	-14.5
2019	CHA	1061	-1.6	-0.2	0.0	-1.8

too much to just regurgitate what could be gleaned from a stat line, and the last decade has dumped a lot of nuance into our laps, there are some hurdles between now and Collins putting his signature on a 15-year lease for a condo in Chicago worth noting: Strikeout rates looming on the fringes of acceptability in the minors tend to only worsen at higher levels. The still-present hitch in his swing figures to get tested by top velocity as he progresses. And the confidence with which advanced pitchers do so figures to have a sharp correlation with how sticky that elite walk rate proves to be. All these, and he still has to continue to progress defensively to prove he's a catcher, the biggest question mark he faced on his draft day. Still, though, power-hitting catcher who walks a ton: It's not a bad starter kit.

YEAR	TEAM	LVL	AGE	PA	DRC+	VORP	BABIP	BRR	FRAA	WARP
2016	WNS	A+	21	153	155	10.8	.333	-0.4	C(18): -0.6	0.8
2017	WNS	A+	22	426	119	22.9	.282	-2.6	C(76): 1.5	1.5
2017	BIR	AA	22	45	156	4.8	.286	-0.1	C(11): -2.4	0.1
2018	BIR	AA	23	531	124	33.7	.329	-3.2	C(74): -14.4	0.3
2019	CHA	MLB	24	29	65	0.0	.244	-0.1	C -2	-0.2

Ryan Cordell   OF

Born: 03/31/92   Age: 27   Bats: R   Throws: R
Height: 6'4"   Weight: 195   Origin: Round 11, 2013 Draft (#340 overall)

YEAR	TEAM	LVL	AGE	PA	R	2B	3B	HR	RBI	BB	K	SB	CS	AVG/OBP/SLG
2016	FRI	AA	24	445	69	22	5	19	70	32	97	12	4	.264/.319/.484
2017	CSP	AAA	25	292	49	18	5	10	45	25	65	9	4	.284/.349/.506
2018	CHR	AAA	26	193	15	9	2	3	22	11	44	7	2	.239/.281/.364
2018	CHA	MLB	26	40	3	1	0	1	4	0	15	0	0	.108/.125/.216
2019	CHA	MLB	27	134	14	6	1	4	15	7	36	3	1	.216/.261/.376

Breakout: 4%   Improve: 32%   Collapse: 6%   Attrition: 25%   MLB: 43%
Comparables: Matt Carson, Brandon Barnes, Slade Heathcott

Getting traded into a White Sox rebuild that has witnessed some of the worst outfield production in recent memory should have been the equivalent of smashing open a window of opportunity with a sledgehammer. Instead, little hiccups like a fractured vertebrae and a broken collarbone conspired to limit Cordell to a 19-game major league cameo, and the rookie passed through eight of those 19 before his first career hit. That decisive blast into the mostly empty left field seats at Camden Yards served as one of the few triumphs in a season that saw Cordell struggle to stake any claim on a center field job that looked like it could have been his throughout spring training, and firmly place himself outside of the White Sox Opening Day roster picture going into 2019. With his 27th birthday coming near Opening Day, the promise of his all-around tools can spark only so much optimism.

YEAR	TEAM	LVL	AGE	PA	DRC+	VORP	BABIP	BRR	FRAA	WARP
2016	FRI	AA	24	445	111	24.7	.299	0.6	CF(42): 3.7, LF(35): 3.8	1.8
2017	CSP	AAA	25	292	102	12.3	.339	1.6	RF(29): 0.0, LF(15): 0.2	0.6
2018	CHR	AAA	26	193	79	-0.1	.293	0.4	CF(22): -0.2, RF(13): -0.4	0.2
2018	CHA	MLB	26	40	61	-3.4	.130	0.4	RF(9): -0.3, CF(7): -0.6	-0.1
2019	CHA	MLB	27	134	70	-0.2	.260	0.2	LF 2, CF 0	0.2

Nicky Delmonico LF

Born: 07/12/92   Age: 26   Bats: L   Throws: R
Height: 6'3"   Weight: 230   Origin: Round 6, 2011 Draft (#185 overall)

YEAR	TEAM	LVL	AGE	PA	R	2B	3B	HR	RBI	BB	K	SB	CS	AVG/OBP/SLG
2016	BIR	AA	23	159	25	14	2	10	31	13	33	1	0	.338/.397/.676
2016	CHR	AAA	23	295	32	16	0	7	30	29	74	2	0	.246/.320/.388
2017	CHR	AAA	24	429	55	18	3	12	45	46	73	4	2	.262/.347/.421
2017	CHA	MLB	24	166	25	4	0	9	23	23	31	2	0	.262/.373/.482
2018	CHA	MLB	25	318	31	11	5	8	25	27	80	1	2	.215/.296/.373
2019	CHA	MLB	26	275	29	11	2	8	31	25	64	1	1	.229/.307/.388

Breakout: 13%   Improve: 44%   Collapse: 11%   Attrition: 22%   MLB: 83%
Comparables: Ben Gamel, Ryan Langerhans, Desmond Jennings

Surprise breakout performances from long-overlooked prospects are utterly delightful, undercut only by their unfortunate tendency to disappear back into obscurity as quickly as they arise. Delmonico was having a hard enough time repeating his surprising late-2017 power surge by mid-May, at the moment Matt Moore missed his target on a 1-2 count by matter of feet and broke the third metacarpal in Delmonico's right hand. Strangely enough, after missing two months of action with a hand injury, the week of his initial return was one of the few stretches where Delmonico flashed signs of carving out space for himself as a potential regular. The rest of the year he was a converted third baseman trying to make it work out in left field, providing decidedly below-average offense while Eloy Jimenez lingered a level below. It's a tenuous spot to be in.

YEAR	TEAM	LVL	AGE	PA	DRC+	VORP	BABIP	BRR	FRAA	WARP
2016	BIR	AA	23	159	179	15.7	.384	-4.3	1B(30): 0.4, 3B(3): 0.1	0.8
2016	CHR	AAA	23	295	95	3.4	.311	-1.8	3B(39): 0.4, RF(17): 0.5	0.3
2017	CHR	AAA	24	429	116	20.5	.296	2.9	3B(73): -1.4, LF(13): -0.6	1.6
2017	CHA	MLB	24	166	120	10.0	.277	0.9	LF(27): 2.8, 1B(4): -0.6	1.1
2018	CHA	MLB	25	318	82	-1.4	.269	-0.7	LF(76): -1.2, 1B(7): 0.6	-0.1
2019	CHA	MLB	26	275	88	2.5	.273	-0.2	1B 0, RF 0	0.2

Luis Gonzalez CF

Born: 09/10/95   Age: 23   Bats: L   Throws: L
Height: 6'1"   Weight: 185   Origin: Round 3, 2017 Draft (#87 overall)

YEAR	TEAM	LVL	AGE	PA	R	2B	3B	HR	RBI	BB	K	SB	CS	AVG/OBP/SLG
2017	KAN	A	21	277	26	13	4	2	12	38	50	2	3	.245/.356/.361
2018	KAN	A	22	255	35	16	2	8	26	21	57	7	2	.300/.358/.491
2018	WNS	A+	22	288	50	24	3	6	45	27	46	3	5	.313/.376/.504
2019	CHA	MLB	23	251	25	8	1	6	22	16	62	1	1	.188/.241/.310

Breakout: 5%   Improve: 22%   Collapse: 1%   Attrition: 10%   MLB: 28%
Comparables: Jake Cave, Johnny Field, Michael Hermosillo

If his college run had ended more smoothly, Gonzalez might have been a first-round pick. Had he been a first-round pick in 2017, it's possible he would not have been buried in Low-A Kannapolis to start the season. Had he not started out there, perhaps his dominant 2018 campaign would be viewed less as a polished and mature college star nuking overwhelmed younger competition, and would have more unambiguously placed him on the prospect map with a clear role in the White Sox future plans. Instead, things are as they are, and the lefty-swinging center fielder who deserved a shot at Double-A this year will be only now be getting his first taste of the high minors. It's easy enough to see him in the majors one day not too long from now, but it's less certain how much his pop and center-field prowess will still be ahead of that of his peers by then.

YEAR	TEAM	LVL	AGE	PA	DRC+	VORP	BABIP	BRR	FRAA	WARP
2017	KAN	A	21	277	115	11.3	.302	-0.2	CF(31): -2.9, LF(18): -0.1	0.3
2018	KAN	A	22	255	145	19.8	.365	-0.6	CF(39): -1.0, RF(13): -1.9	1.1
2018	WNS	A+	22	288	145	26.8	.354	5.8	CF(31): 3.9, LF(14): 0.2	2.5
2019	CHA	MLB	23	251	45	-8.3	.223	-0.4	CF 1, RF 0	-0.8

Eloy Jimenez   LF

Born: 11/27/96   Age: 22   Bats: R   Throws: R
Height: 6'4"   Weight: 205   Origin: International Free Agent, 2013

YEAR	TEAM	LVL	AGE	PA	R	2B	3B	HR	RBI	BB	K	SB	CS	AVG/OBP/SLG
2016	SBN	A	19	464	65	40	3	14	81	25	94	8	3	.329/.369/.532
2017	MYR	A+	20	174	23	6	2	8	32	18	35	0	0	.271/.351/.490
2017	WNS	A+	20	122	20	11	1	8	26	12	21	0	2	.345/.410/.682
2017	BIR	AA	20	73	11	5	0	3	7	5	16	1	1	.353/.397/.559
2018	BIR	AA	21	228	36	15	2	10	42	18	39	0	0	.317/.368/.556
2018	CHR	AAA	21	228	28	13	1	12	33	14	30	0	1	.355/.399/.597
2019	CHA	MLB	22	461	56	23	1	19	62	24	93	0	0	.278/.319/.469

Breakout: 17%   Improve: 51%   Collapse: 1%   Attrition: 14%   MLB: 63%
Comparables: Oswaldo Arcia, Austin Hays, Joel Guzman

Jimenez is not particularly fleet of foot. He's a large young man built like a Mack truck and no one expects those things to go from 0-to-60 mph particularly quickly either. As precocious as he is offensively, he's more of a normal large-bodied 22-year-old corner outfielder when it comes to his defense. He seemed to lose interest in walking during this past year against vastly inferior and overmatched minor league pitching, but also seemed to lose all interest in striking out, so call it even. If all these criticisms feel sort of like forced and insufficient explanations for why Jimenez—blatantly one of the most polished and big league-ready bats in the minors all season long—did not make his major league debut, then this served as a good synthesis of what it was like to follow his 2018 campaign. He is going to hit, hit and hit. He is going to do it nigh-immediately and he is not going to do much else, but he is going to do it enough that no one cares about much else either.

YEAR	TEAM	LVL	AGE	PA	DRC+	VORP	BABIP	BRR	FRAA	WARP
2016	SBN	A	19	464	160	35.7	.391	-0.3	LF(86): -4.6, RF(11): 0.4	2.9
2017	MYR	A+	20	174	155	10.1	.304	-0.3	LF(17): 0.3, RF(7): -0.1	1.0
2017	WNS	A+	20	122	155	14.1	.370	0.4	RF(21): -0.6	0.7
2017	BIR	AA	20	73	160	9.0	.429	0.1	RF(15): -1.1	0.4
2018	BIR	AA	21	228	158	23.9	.344	-1.3	LF(30): -3.6, RF(13): -1.8	0.7
2018	CHR	AAA	21	228	170	19.9	.371	-1.8	LF(41): -0.2, RF(6): 0.0	1.8
2019	CHA	MLB	22	461	113	20.2	.316	-1.0	LF -1, RF -1	1.8

Nick Madrigal   2B

Born: 03/05/97   Age: 22   Bats: R   Throws: R
Height: 5'7"   Weight: 165   Origin: Round 1, 2018 Draft (#4 overall)

YEAR	TEAM	LVL	AGE	PA	R	2B	3B	HR	RBI	BB	K	SB	CS	AVG/OBP/SLG
2018	KAN	A	21	49	9	3	0	0	6	1	0	2	2	.341/.347/.409
2018	WNS	A+	21	107	14	4	0	0	9	5	5	6	3	.306/.355/.347
2019	CHA	MLB	22	251	24	7	0	5	23	6	37	6	3	.232/.258/.319

Breakout: 17%   Improve: 25%   Collapse: 0%   Attrition: 19%   MLB: 26%
Comparables: Breyvic Valera, Alexi Amarista, Yolmer Sanchez

Despite being a do-everything, ego-less infielder generously listed at 5'7" and defined primarily by his categorical refusal to ever strike out, Madrigal was not actually created in a lab funded by a shady cabal of color commentators over 60 filled with resentment over the direction of the game these days. Despite being a diminutive figure with an increasingly unique quirk that defines his game, Madrigal is not a gimmick player, but rather the fourth-overall pick from last June's draft and a top-50 prospect in the game. His extreme contact ability is as clearly his carrying tool as light tower home run power or 100 mph fastball velocity would be for the average prospect, and even at the end of a long season filled with a broken wrist, a national championship at Oregon State, and a Carolina League playoff run in Winston-Salem, it was on display in his pro debut. Not much in the way of the extra-base pop the White Sox touted on draft night, nor the willingness to end a plate appearance with some other result than putting a ball in play were on display, but the cabal can wait for those details.

YEAR	TEAM	LVL	AGE	PA	DRC+	VORP	BABIP	BRR	FRAA	WARP
2018	KAN	A	21	49	143	5.3	.319	1.1	2B(12): 0.9	0.5
2018	WNS	A+	21	107	120	2.7	.319	0.0	2B(25): -1.8	0.1
2019	CHA	MLB	22	251	58	-4.4	.256	-0.2	2B -2, SS 0	-0.7

Luis Robert CF

Born: 08/03/97   Age: 21   Bats: R   Throws: R
Height: 6'3"   Weight: 185   Origin: International Free Agent, 2017

YEAR	TEAM	LVL	AGE	PA	R	2B	3B	HR	RBI	BB	K	SB	CS	AVG/OBP/SLG
2017	DWS	RK	19	114	17	8	1	3	14	22	23	12	3	.310/.491/.536
2018	KAN	A	20	50	5	3	1	0	4	4	12	4	2	.289/.360/.400
2018	WNS	A+	20	140	21	6	1	0	11	8	37	8	2	.244/.317/.309
2019	CHA	MLB	21	251	28	11	0	5	19	17	81	8	2	.182/.255/.292

Breakout: 1%   Improve: 1%   Collapse: 0%   Attrition: 1%   MLB: 1%
Comparables: Joe Benson, Xavier Avery, Abraham Almonte

When Luis Robert was signed to great fanfare, the public had little to identify him beyond nutty and precocious Serie Nacional stats, grainy batting practice video, and excited reports from clandestine showcases. And yet, more than a year later, Luis Robert's legend remains largely theoretical. Just the sight of his long, lean and muscled frame jogging around for five minutes gives a glimpse as why someone paid $26 million to bring him to their camp, and it takes only a couple batting practice cuts to see what the most standout offering of an electric toolset is. But after missing roughly three months of his first stateside season with two separate left thumb sprains, the wait for him to get in rhythm and show his in-game power has encompassed his entire professional career. It's been impressive to see how much he can make do with plus speed and no fear on the basepaths, and a strong Arizona Fall League quieted some concerns over the whiff-heavy nature of his Single-A struggles. But the primary hope for Luis Robert in 2019 is to actually see Luis Robert.

YEAR	TEAM	LVL	AGE	PA	DRC+	VORP	BABIP	BRR	FRAA	WARP
2017	DWS	RK	19	114	206	21.7	.397	2.5	CF(19): -0.5	1.5
2018	KAN	A	20	50	105	3.0	.394	-0.2	CF(10): 0.0	0.0
2018	WNS	A+	20	140	84	2.7	.341	0.5	CF(27): 3.1, RF(4): -0.4	0.2
2019	CHA	MLB	21	251	52	-5.1	.258	0.5	CF 2, RF 0	-0.3

Blake Rutherford OF

Born: 05/02/97   Age: 22   Bats: L   Throws: R
Height: 6'3"   Weight: 195   Origin: Round 1, 2016 Draft (#18 overall)

YEAR	TEAM	LVL	AGE	PA	R	2B	3B	HR	RBI	BB	K	SB	CS	AVG/OBP/SLG
2016	YAT	RK	19	30	3	1	0	1	3	4	6	0	0	.240/.333/.400
2016	PUL	RK	19	100	13	7	4	2	9	9	24	0	2	.382/.440/.618
2017	CSC	A	20	304	41	20	2	2	30	25	55	9	4	.281/.342/.391
2017	KAN	A	20	136	11	5	0	0	5	13	21	1	0	.213/.289/.254
2018	WNS	A+	21	487	67	25	9	7	78	34	90	15	8	.293/.345/.436
2019	CHA	MLB	22	251	20	8	1	5	24	9	69	2	1	.193/.220/.304

Breakout: 4%   Improve: 7%   Collapse: 0%   Attrition: 6%   MLB: 8%
Comparables: Jorge Bonifacio, Destin Hood, Rymer Liriano

All the smart baseball people out there seem to insist that context matters. As someone who entered 2018 coming off a truly abysmal second half at Low-A Kannapolis that nearly dragged him clear off every top-100 prospect list, Rutherford undertook an impressive bounce-back campaign. Moving to a more hitter-friendly ballpark, he more than tripled his previous year's home run output, flirted with a .300 average all year while showing actual gap power, as opposed to when we just say "gap power" to speak nicely about guys who can't hit home runs. He did this even though the Sox promoted him after a season that could have merited a repeat year in Kannapolis, at an age where most college prospects would be getting their first taste of professional baseball and would be happy to hold their own in the Carolina League. All of that is pretty good work for one year. In another context, as a lauded former first-round pick, as the centerpiece of a seven-player deal, as a top-100 prospect, he could be a corner outfielder with moderate power and a pedestrian on-base percentage. This would sound better if the downside was written first.

YEAR	TEAM	LVL	AGE	PA	DRC+	VORP	BABIP	BRR	FRAA	WARP
2016	YAT	RK	19	30	108	2.8	.263	0.0	CF(6): -1.1	-0.1
2016	PUL	RK	19	100	178	14.7	.500	0.0	CF(14): -1.7, LF(2): -0.2	0.4
2017	CSC	A	20	304	99	11.0	.341	-2.6	CF(39): -5.6, LF(13): -0.5	-0.8
2017	KAN	A	20	136	98	-4.8	.257	-0.1	CF(13): -1.3, LF(10): -0.3	-0.1
2018	WNS	A+	21	487	120	18.7	.351	1.1	RF(74): -2.5, LF(15): -2.7	0.4
2019	CHA	MLB	22	251	32	-13.4	.243	0.0	RF 0, LF -1	-1.6

Steele Walker CF

Born: 07/30/96   Age: 22   Bats: L   Throws: L
Height: 5'11"   Weight: 190   Origin: Round 2, 2018 Draft (#46 overall)

YEAR	TEAM	LVL	AGE	PA	R	2B	3B	HR	RBI	BB	K	SB	CS	AVG/OBP/SLG
2018	GRF	RK	21	38	4	1	0	2	4	1	7	1	1	.206/.263/.412
2018	KAN	A	21	126	13	5	0	3	17	8	29	5	1	.186/.246/.310
2019	CHA	MLB	22	251	18	5	0	7	22	6	73	2	1	.121/.145/.225

Breakout: 3%   Improve: 3%   Collapse: 0%   Attrition: 3%   MLB: 4%
Comparables: Darrell Ceciliani, Michael Taylor, Aaron Altherr

Every year, there just has to be a Day 1 draft pick who perfectly embodies the principle of not judging college players by their immediate pro debuts. Placed into action after straining his right oblique near the tail end of a breakout junior season at Oklahoma, a rusty and weary Walker hit absolutely nothing across three separate stops. Given a fresh start in 2019, it'll be up to the 22-year-old to define which of his wide array of potentially average tools (power being the standout) will play up in games. He might not be a plus offensive contributor, he might not stick in center field, but if he shows progress toward at least one, he'll probably get another full writeup in the next version of this book.

YEAR	TEAM	LVL	AGE	PA	DRC+	VORP	BABIP	BRR	FRAA	WARP
2018	GRF	RK	21	38	74	0.9	.192	0.4	CF(8): -2.0	-0.2
2018	KAN	A	21	126	58	-1.3	.214	0.3	CF(21): 1.2	-0.3
2019	CHA	MLB	22	251	-6	-23.0	.138	0.1	CF 0, RF 0	-2.4

Seby Zavala C

Born: 08/28/93   Age: 25   Bats: R   Throws: R
Height: 5'11"   Weight: 215   Origin: Round 12, 2015 Draft (#352 overall)

YEAR	TEAM	LVL	AGE	PA	R	2B	3B	HR	RBI	BB	K	SB	CS	AVG/OBP/SLG
2016	KAN	A	22	404	40	19	3	7	49	35	108	1	1	.253/.330/.381
2017	KAN	A	23	207	32	8	0	13	34	13	52	0	0	.259/.327/.514
2017	WNS	A+	23	228	31	13	0	8	38	24	52	1	0	.302/.376/.485
2018	BIR	AA	24	232	32	7	0	11	31	27	65	0	0	.271/.358/.472
2018	CHR	AAA	24	191	18	15	0	2	20	6	44	0	2	.243/.267/.359
2019	CHA	MLB	25	58	6	3	0	2	6	3	17	0	0	.222/.263/.389

Breakout: 5%   Improve: 19%   Collapse: 0%   Attrition: 18%   MLB: 29%
Comparables: Luke Montz, Andrew Knapp, Johnny Monell

As a San Diego State product of a certain era, Zavala has a requisite Tony Gwynn tattoo and a variety of oft-used phrases from his old college coach that he trots out when appropriate. One of them is "Know who you is,"

YEAR	TEAM	P. COUNT	FRM RUNS	BLK RUNS	THRW RUNS	TOT RUNS
2018	BIR	4264	3.3	0.1	0.4	4.0
2018	CHR	4728	-2.6	0.0	-0.1	-2.3
2019	CHA	2122	-0.8	-0.1	-0.1	-1.0

which probably sounded better coming from the mouth of a man with 3,141 career big league hits than it reads in print, but fits Zavala himself surprisingly well. As a short and stout, slow-footed catcher with a surgically repaired elbow, he's not in this book because he dazzles with tools, but more for his ability to actualize everything he has in games. He doesn't have all-fields power, but is proficient at tucking in his wrists and yanking the ball to left with authority. He doesn't have a cannon or block pitches particularly well, but Zavala makes a concerted effort to frame and calls a game like someone who listened to Tony Gwynn talk a lot. At 25 years of age and having yet to solve Triple-A, it's hard to see him as the White Sox catcher of the future, but he'll likely be a White Sox catcher of the present before long.

YEAR	TEAM	LVL	AGE	PA	DRC+	VORP	BABIP	BRR	FRAA	WARP
2016	KAN	A	22	404	105	17.9	.341	-1.3	C(92): -1.3	1.0
2017	KAN	A	23	207	131	17.6	.289	0.9	C(43): -1.5	1.2
2017	WNS	A+	23	228	139	20.6	.373	3.0	C(34): 0.9	1.7
2018	BIR	AA	24	232	133	18.4	.339	0.0	C(31): 4.0	1.5
2018	CHR	AAA	24	191	81	-2.5	.304	-1.2	C(35): -3.0	-0.4
2019	CHA	MLB	25	58	69	0.5	.283	-0.1	C -1	-0.1

Spencer Adams   RHP

Born: 04/13/96   Age: 23   Bats: R   Throws: R
Height: 6'3"   Weight: 171   Origin: Round 2, 2014 Draft (#44 overall)

YEAR	TEAM	LVL	AGE	W	L	SV	G	GS	IP	H	HR	BB/9	K/9	K	GB%	BABIP
2016	WNS	A+	20	8	7	0	18	18	107²	120	7	1.8	6.2	74	55%	.313
2016	BIR	AA	20	2	5	0	9	9	55¹	59	2	1.6	4.2	26	42%	.298
2017	BIR	AA	21	7	15	0	26	26	152²	171	19	2.4	6.7	113	49%	.314
2018	BIR	AA	22	3	6	0	13	13	68¹	80	10	2.6	6.9	53	44%	.329
2018	CHR	AAA	22	4	7	0	15	15	90¹	82	10	3.8	4.2	42	42%	.256
2019	CHA	MLB	23	1	1	0	3	3	15	17	3	3.1	6.3	10	44%	.294

Breakout: 2%   Improve: 6%   Collapse: 5%   Attrition: 9%   MLB: 11%
Comparables: Adrian Sampson, Trevor Oaks, Ryan Sherriff

For a year where he mostly pitched in a manner completely antithetical to his core principles as a ballplayer, Spencer Adams didn't have a half-bad 2018. Reaching Triple-A and not getting hammered there is fine work for a prospect defined by strike-throwing and pitchability more than overpowering stuff. That it came alongside a career-high and objectively high walk rate while his velocity languished in the low-90s was more worrisome. He never looked quite like his fluid, athletic, can-still-dunk-if-you-get-him-on-the-court self outside the month in Birmingham that got him promoted. Adams will not turn 23 until April and is already a step away from the majors, so 2019 is hardly a crossroads in his career. But prospects like him make their money by providing metronome-like consistency, not by suddenly having their command click to unlock wipeout stuff, so the control problems need to be a short blip in his ascent.

YEAR	TEAM	LVL	AGE	WHIP	ERA	DRA	WARP	MPH	FB%	WHF	CSP
2016	WNS	A+	20	1.31	4.01	3.57	2.3				
2016	BIR	AA	20	1.25	3.90	3.62	1.0				
2017	BIR	AA	21	1.38	4.42	5.58	-0.8				
2018	BIR	AA	22	1.46	4.59	7.01	-1.3				
2018	CHR	AAA	22	1.33	3.19	5.23	0.3				
2019	CHA	MLB	23	1.49	5.16	5.58	0.0				

Dylan Cease RHP

Born: 12/28/95   Age: 23   Bats: R   Throws: R
Height: 6'2"   Weight: 190   Origin: Round 6, 2014 Draft (#169 overall)

YEAR	TEAM	LVL	AGE	W	L	SV	G	GS	IP	H	HR	BB/9	K/9	K	GB%	BABIP
2016	EUG	A-	20	2	0	0	12	12	44²	27	1	5.0	13.3	66	55%	.295
2017	SBN	A	21	1	2	0	13	13	51²	39	2	4.5	12.9	74	46%	.339
2017	KAN	A	21	0	8	0	9	9	41²	35	1	3.9	11.2	52	43%	.330
2018	WNS	A+	22	9	2	0	13	13	71²	52	5	3.5	10.3	82	50%	.273
2018	BIR	AA	22	3	0	0	10	10	52¹	30	3	3.8	13.4	78	50%	.273
2019	CHA	MLB	23	2	2	0	20	5	41	34	4	5.4	10.9	50	43%	.295

Breakout: 12%   Improve: 20%   Collapse: 17%   Attrition: 25%   MLB: 42%
Comparables: Zack Wheeler, Stephen Gonsalves, Carl Edwards Jr.

In his second to last start of the season, Dylan Cease needed 40 pitches to labor through the first inning on a rainy mid-August night. Since he was already near his season innings limit, the White Sox just pulled him. He got knocked around in his first game after being promoted to Double-A, even while striking out seven in less than five innings. He was absolutely torched for eight runs on nine hits in the middle of May when he was still at Winston-Salem—he explained that he just didn't have it that day. That's about half the comment space accounted for, but it was more concise to detail all the times Cease wasn't overpowering against minor league competition in 2018 rather than vice versa. Always blessed with top shelf velocity and an occasionally jaw-dropping curveball, Cease was finally challenged with a real starter's workload and responded with a dominant and healthy year. After a grip tip from James Shields in spring gave him more command of his curve, his best outings found him with an effective changeup, along with an occasional slider. There's still a gulf between his current command level and what will allow him to be consistent in the majors, and there's a logic that someone with his stuff was never going to be tested at the lower levels. But he'll be in the mix to be a top-50 prospect going into 2019, and he's earned it.

YEAR	TEAM	LVL	AGE	WHIP	ERA	DRA	WARP	MPH	FB%	WHF	CSP
2016	EUG	A-	20	1.16	2.22	3.00	1.2				
2017	SBN	A	21	1.26	2.79	3.50	1.1				
2017	KAN	A	21	1.27	3.89	3.00	1.1				
2018	WNS	A+	22	1.12	2.89	2.90	2.0				
2018	BIR	AA	22	0.99	1.72	2.77	1.6				
2019	CHA	MLB	23	1.43	4.07	4.38	0.4				

Dane Dunning   RHP

Born: 12/20/94   Age: 24   Bats: R   Throws: R
Height: 6'4"   Weight: 200   Origin: Round 1, 2016 Draft (#29 overall)

YEAR	TEAM	LVL	AGE	W	L	SV	G	GS	IP	H	HR	BB/9	K/9	K	GB%	BABIP
2016	AUB	A-	21	3	2	0	7	7	33²	26	1	1.9	7.8	29	65%	.263
2017	KAN	A	22	2	0	0	4	4	26	13	0	0.7	11.4	33	64%	.224
2017	WNS	A+	22	6	8	0	22	22	118	114	15	2.7	10.3	135	52%	.316
2018	WNS	A+	23	1	1	0	4	4	24¹	20	2	1.1	11.5	31	61%	.300
2018	BIR	AA	23	5	2	0	11	11	62	57	0	3.3	10.0	69	49%	.343
2019	CHA	MLB	24	4	6	0	15	15	80¹	79	11	3.3	8.8	79	48%	.304

Breakout: 13%   Improve: 26%   Collapse: 14%   Attrition: 30%   MLB: 45%
Comparables: Jordan Montgomery, Sean Nolin, Cody Martin

Despite whatever notions his profile photo and thick-rimmed black glasses at the center of it might carry, despite what images the description of "back-end-to-mid-rotation starter who thrives on plus command" might conjure, Dunning is a physically imposing figure. He stands a strong, thickly-built 6'4" with all the muscle and athleticism to hold his delivery through the rigors of a full season. But despite his reputation as a safe and reliable starting pitching prospect—as safe and reliable as those can be—Dunning was still felled by the injury bug in 2018. He labored through whispers of elbow pain until they became a full-throated shout, and a sprain ended his season in late June, though he did complete a rehab circuit without any setbacks and still expects to avoid surgery. There may or may not be such a thing as a pitching prospect, but there's definitely no such thing as a hurt pitching prospect.

YEAR	TEAM	LVL	AGE	WHIP	ERA	DRA	WARP	MPH	FB%	WHF	CSP
2016	AUB	A-	21	0.98	2.14	3.92	0.5				
2017	KAN	A	22	0.58	0.35	3.10	0.7				
2017	WNS	A+	22	1.27	3.51	4.05	1.7				
2018	WNS	A+	23	0.95	2.59	3.51	0.5				
2018	BIR	AA	23	1.29	2.76	3.58	1.3				
2019	CHA	MLB	24	1.36	4.36	4.58	0.8				

Caleb Frare   LHP

Born: 07/08/93   Age: 25   Bats: L   Throws: L
Height: 6'1"   Weight: 210   Origin: Round 11, 2012 Draft (#367 overall)

YEAR	TEAM	LVL	AGE	W	L	SV	G	GS	IP	H	HR	BB/9	K/9	K	GB%	BABIP
2016	TAM	A+	22	3	3	0	32	0	49	33	0	4.2	9.6	52	56%	.275
2017	TRN	AA	23	2	2	0	24	0	33²	19	2	9.1	11.2	42	48%	.254
2017	TAM	A+	23	1	2	1	15	0	29	29	4	5.6	11.2	36	43%	.379
2018	TRN	AA	24	4	1	5	31	0	43²	25	1	3.1	11.7	57	39%	.258
2018	CHR	AAA	24	1	0	0	11	0	12²	5	0	5.0	13.5	19	42%	.208
2018	CHA	MLB	24	0	1	0	11	0	7	6	0	5.1	11.6	9	29%	.353
2019	CHA	MLB	25	2	2	0	36	0	37²	33	5	5.6	10.9	46	43%	.300

Breakout: 21%   Improve: 26%   Collapse: 13%   Attrition: 28%   MLB: 44%
Comparables: James Pazos, Kevin Quackenbush, Shawn Armstrong

Frare's knowledge of R-rated movies that came out before he was 17 has proven strong in limited testing, but it's likely he's unfamiliar with Samuel L. Jackson's portrayal of Mitch Henessey in The Long Kiss Goodnight. Particularly so his line cautioning Charlie Baltimore, played by Geena Davis, that it isn't so easy to leave New Jersey: "Others have tried and failed. The entire population in fact." With that in mind, and that Frare walked 34 batters in 33 2/3 innings during his 2017 stint there, Frare's escape from Double-A Trenton is doubly impressive. Thanks to the revolutionary new method of "throwing the ball as hard as I can," he drastically cut his walk rate, and indeed, throws harder, sitting in the mid-90s and touching 97. Control eluded him during his big league cameo in September, but his deceptive arm action and slider could power him to a role as a lefty specialist for years to come.

YEAR	TEAM	LVL	AGE	WHIP	ERA	DRA	WARP	MPH	FB%	WHF	CSP
2016	TAM	A+	22	1.14	0.92	2.16	1.6				
2017	TRN	AA	23	1.57	4.28	3.82	0.4				
2017	TAM	A+	23	1.62	3.72	3.50	0.5				
2018	TRN	AA	24	0.92	0.62	2.62	1.2				
2018	CHR	AAA	24	0.95	0.71	2.50	0.4				
2018	CHA	MLB	24	1.43	5.14	2.03	0.2	96.3	54.3	17.8	42.6
2019	CHA	MLB	25	1.51	4.74	4.89	0.1	96.0	55.6	18.3	43.7

Alec Hansen   RHP

Born: 10/10/94   Age: 24   Bats: R   Throws: R
Height: 6'7"   Weight: 235   Origin: Round 2, 2016 Draft (#49 overall)

YEAR	TEAM	LVL	AGE	W	L	SV	G	GS	IP	H	HR	BB/9	K/9	K	GB%	BABIP
2016	WSX	RK	21	0	0	0	3	3	7	1	0	5.1	14.1	11	70%	.100
2016	GRF	RK	21	2	0	0	7	7	36²	12	3	2.9	14.5	59	52%	.161
2016	KAN	A	21	0	1	0	2	2	11	11	0	3.3	9.0	11	53%	.344
2017	KAN	A	22	7	3	0	13	13	72²	57	3	2.8	11.4	92	32%	.292
2017	WNS	A+	22	4	5	0	11	11	58¹	42	5	3.9	12.7	82	38%	.296
2017	BIR	AA	22	0	0	0	2	2	10¹	15	0	2.6	14.8	17	36%	.536
2018	BIR	AA	23	0	4	0	9	9	35²	30	3	10.6	8.8	35	33%	.293
2018	WNS	A+	23	0	1	0	5	5	15²	14	0	9.8	11.5	20	27%	.378
2019	CHA	MLB	24	2	5	0	12	12	56¹	54	9	7.1	10.1	63	38%	.304

Breakout: 6%   Improve: 9%   Collapse: 7%   Attrition: 13%   MLB: 19%
Comparables: Humberto Sanchez, Josh Collmenter, Austin Brice

"At least he stayed healthy" would be a decent qualifier to throw out after a year of disappointing performance for a top pitching prospect. Conversely, a season completely lost to injury would at least have preserved the optimism and dominance of Alec Hansen's 2017 campaign until February of 2019. Instead he was denied both silver linings, missing the first half of 2018 with a strangely nagging forearm issue and missing his spots for all of a nightmarish second half. The imposing right-hander was a top-50 prospect coming into the year, openly discussing his expectation to make it in the majors by September, and he ended the season still ineffective after a demotion to the Carolina League. Normally it would be fatuous to wonder if someone walking over a batter per inning at High-A at age 23 could turn it around and become a big league starter, but Hansen's biggest solace is that he's been here before, and worked his way back after a similarly walk-addled junior season at Oklahoma. That's if you consider that solace, though.

YEAR	TEAM	LVL	AGE	WHIP	ERA	DRA	WARP	MPH	FB%	WHF	CSP
2016	WSX	RK	21	0.71	0.00	2.03	0.3				
2016	GRF	RK	21	0.65	1.23	1.92	1.5				
2016	KAN	A	21	1.36	2.45	2.40	0.4				
2017	KAN	A	22	1.10	2.48	2.80	2.1				
2017	WNS	A+	22	1.15	2.93	3.42	1.3				
2017	BIR	AA	22	1.74	4.35	2.95	0.3				
2018	BIR	AA	23	2.02	6.56	5.96	-0.3				
2018	WNS	A+	23	1.98	5.74	4.53	0.1				
2019	CHA	MLB	24	1.75	5.70	6.02	-0.4				

Jordan Stephens   RHP

Born: 09/12/92   Age: 26   Bats: R   Throws: R
Height: 6'1"   Weight: 190   Origin: Round 5, 2015 Draft (#142 overall)

YEAR	TEAM	LVL	AGE	W	L	SV	G	GS	IP	H	HR	BB/9	K/9	K	GB%	BABIP
2016	WNS	A+	23	7	10	0	27	27	141	129	12	3.1	9.9	155	46%	.319
2017	BIR	AA	24	3	7	0	16	16	91^2	84	4	3.4	8.1	83	43%	.309
2018	BIR	AA	25	4	3	0	7	7	39^2	37	1	2.7	9.1	40	37%	.340
2018	CHR	AAA	25	4	7	0	21	21	107	114	11	3.5	8.3	99	34%	.328
2019	CHA	MLB	26	2	3	0	20	5	41	42	7	3.7	8.3	38	39%	.299

Breakout: 7%   Improve: 13%   Collapse: 6%   Attrition: 30%   MLB: 35%
Comparables: Kyle McGowin, Sam LeCure, Hector Ambriz

A good, hard overhand curveball and the knowledge of how to use it is a fine starter kit for a pitching prospect. Stephens' ability to spin it has carried the Rice product to the precipice of the majors despite a myriad of different injuries, a much slighter than typical physical frame, and a pedestrian fastball which can flatten out when he lets his back leg collapse in his delivery. He's 26, doesn't throw hard, his changeup is more of show-me offering and he spent most of 2018 hitting his head in Triple-A, so no one will be forecasting greatness out of the rotation even if he figures to get a crack at the White Sox starting mix in 2019. The beautiful simplicity of his attack when he's pairing high fastballs with the hard vertical drop of his spinner, and their waning effectiveness upon repeat viewings, gives you an idea of where the best moments of his career might take place.

YEAR	TEAM	LVL	AGE	WHIP	ERA	DRA	WARP	MPH	FB%	WHF	CSP
2016	WNS	A+	23	1.26	3.45	2.98	4.0				
2017	BIR	AA	24	1.30	3.14	4.06	1.2				
2018	BIR	AA	25	1.24	2.95	3.79	0.7				
2018	CHR	AAA	25	1.46	4.71	4.77	0.9				
2019	CHA	MLB	26	1.46	5.04	5.25	0.0				

LINEOUTS

Hitters

HITTER	POS	TEAM	LVL	AGE	PA	R	2B	3B	HR	RBI	BB	K	SB	CS	AVG/OBP/SLG	DRC+	WARP
Bryce Bush	3B	WSX	Rk	18	52	8	4	0	1	8	8	4	1	2	.442/.538/.605	238	0.9
	3B	GRF	Rk	18	108	16	5	1	2	10	10	21	3	0	.250/.327/.385	73	-0.3
Luis Curbelo	SS	KAN	A	20	343	35	19	2	3	31	18	87	0	0	.237/.282/.338	81	-0.5
Lency Delgado	3B	WSX	Rk	19	150	20	4	1	1	22	9	40	4	0	.233/.309/.301	58	-0.1
Laz Rivera	SS	KAN	A	23	265	42	15	2	6	24	6	48	7	3	.346/.395/.502	162	2.0
	SS	WNS	A+	23	250	38	15	2	7	37	7	44	10	7	.280/.325/.458	105	0.8
Jose Rondon	SS	CHR	AAA	24	336	41	15	4	18	38	16	82	5	6	.249/.290/.495	98	2.1
	SS	CHA	MLB	24	107	15	6	0	6	14	7	30	2	1	.230/.280/.470	94	0.2
Gavin Sheets	1B	WNS	A+	22	497	58	28	2	6	61	52	81	1	0	.293/.368/.407	132	0.3
Charlie Tilson	CF	CHA	MLB	25	121	7	1	1	0	11	10	20	2	3	.264/.331/.292	72	-0.1
	CF	CHR	AAA	25	292	27	12	0	0	25	16	52	10	2	.244/.288/.289	70	-0.7

Jake Burger entered 2018 ready to answer doubters about his ability to translate his plus raw power into game production and that his burly frame could stick at third base. Instead, he ruptured his left Achilles tendon on two separate occasions, which did little to address either concern. ⓧ The whole business about the $290,000 bonus that the White Sox offered **Bryce Bush** belies the underdog story of a low-round high schooler rolling in and torching complex league ball. He's a strong young man who can put the bat on the ball and hang with pitchers several years older than he is. He'll put those extra few years to good use in finding a defensive position. ⓧ Finally recovered from a meniscus tear than ended his 2017 season after just three games, **Luis Curbelo's** 2018 debut at a full-season affiliate wound up being an introduction to the age-old question: Is it better to be a toolsy but largely unseen prospect resigned to the backfields of the spring training complex, or a toolsy but underperforming prospect treading water in an aggressive assignment? ⓧ **Lency Delgado** proves that the White Sox as an organization are more enraptured by players born in Cuba than they are leery of spending high-round picks on high schoolers. Delgado is listed as a shortstop for now, but he's also listed as 6'3", 215 pounds at age 19, so, c'mon now. ⓧ The only way some 24-year-old pop-up prospect—who hasn't reached Double-A yet and came into pro ball as a 28th-round senior signing—is getting so much as a lineout in the Annual is if they did something drastic like slash .314/.361/.481 across two levels while showing the capability to handle a premium position. Luckily, **Laz Rivera** did that. ⓧ A review of **Jose Rondon**'s comments in previous versions of this publication reveals the story of an agile defender with some mentions of a solid hit tool and next to no home run power to speak of. Yet, in an organization that possessed Eloy Jimenez and Jose Abreu, his 24 home runs across Triple-A and a pair of stints in the majors was more than either one of those dudes managed. ☯ It would be nice if a hitter as smart, multi-faceted and polished in his approach as **Gavin Sheets** could be appreciated beyond the bellows of "WHERE ARE THE DINGERS?" But unfortunately he's a first baseman, so no dice. ☯ After losing the last two months of 2016 and all of 2017 to wave after wave of injuries and misfortune, everyone in the White Sox organization was pleased to see **Charlie Tilson** beat the odds to make it back to the majors. Eventually a sub-.300 slugging percentage caused the good feelings to wane. ☯ One definition of "utility" is "functional rather than attractive." Speaking in baseball terms, **Ramon Torres** is an archetypal utility player: functional middle-infield defense and hitting that—no, really, just look away.

Pitchers

PITCHER	TEAM	LVL	AGE	W	L	SV	G	GS	IP	H	HR	BB/9	K/9	K	GB%	WHIP	ERA	DRA	WARP
Manny Banuelos	OKL	AAA	27	9	7	0	31	18	108²	109	10	3.5	10.5	127	45%	1.39	3.73	2.82	3.3
Aaron Bummer	CHR	AAA	24	2	3	0	31	0	30²	27	0	3.2	8.8	30	67%	1.24	2.64	3.51	0.6
	CHA	MLB	24	0	1	0	37	0	31²	40	1	2.8	9.9	35	62%	1.58	4.26	3.71	0.4
Randall Delgado	RNO	AAA	28	0	1	0	13	1	18	11	1	3.0	7.0	14	35%	0.94	2.00	4.35	0.2
	ARI	MLB	28	2	0	0	10	0	11¹	11	3	4.8	4.0	5	35%	1.50	4.76	5.84	-0.1
Bernardo Flores	WNS	A+	22	5	4	0	12	12	77²	75	5	2.0	6.7	58	56%	1.18	2.55	3.40	1.7
	BIR	AA	22	3	5	0	13	13	78¹	79	5	1.6	5.4	47	52%	1.19	2.76	3.98	1.2
Jordan Guerrero	BIR	AA	24	3	6	0	14	13	65¹	84	6	2.6	8.0	58	43%	1.58	6.06	4.46	0.7
	CHR	AAA	24	7	2	0	12	12	65	64	4	3.9	8.6	62	52%	1.42	3.46	4.12	1.0
Lincoln Henzman	KAN	A	22	6	3	0	13	13	72²	68	5	1.0	7.4	60	62%	1.05	2.23	3.30	1.6
	WNS	A+	22	0	1	0	14	9	34²	34	1	2.6	5.2	20	56%	1.27	2.60	3.71	0.6
Tyler Johnson	KAN	A	22	5	0	7	20	0	27	16	1	3.3	15.3	46	56%	0.96	1.33	1.96	0.9
	WNS	A+	22	4	0	7	21	0	31	19	1	1.7	12.5	43	44%	0.81	1.45	2.52	0.9
Jimmy Lambert	WNS	A+	23	5	7	0	13	13	70²	57	5	2.7	10.2	80	46%	1.10	3.95	3.18	1.8
	BIR	AA	23	3	1	0	5	5	25	20	2	2.2	10.8	30	40%	1.04	2.88	2.69	0.8
Evan Marshall	CLE	MLB	28	0	0	0	10	0	7	12	0	5.1	11.6	9	56%	2.29	7.71	3.65	0.1
	COH	AAA	28	1	1	4	20	0	24	18	1	1.1	7.9	21	68%	0.88	1.12	4.06	0.3
Kodi Medeiros	BLX	AA	22	7	5	0	20	15	103¹	90	9	3.9	9.3	107	50%	1.31	3.14	4.35	1.1
	BIR	AA	22	0	2	0	7	7	34¹	31	4	5.8	8.9	34	53%	1.54	4.98	4.33	0.4
Josh Osich	SFN	MLB	29	0	0	0	12	0	12	20	2	5.2	7.5	10	45%	2.25	8.25	6.64	-0.2
	SAC	AAA	29	0	0	0	37	2	45¹	56	2	3.6	8.3	42	47%	1.63	4.96	3.99	0.6
Konnor Pilkington	GRF	Rk	20	0	1	0	6	6	12	14	1	3.0	6.8	9	52%	1.50	5.25	4.36	0.2
Jose Ruiz	WNS	A+	23	0	0	2	10	0	13¹	6	2	3.4	14.9	22	33%	0.82	2.70	2.86	0.3
	BIR	AA	23	3	1	14	33	0	45¹	33	2	3.8	10.9	55	41%	1.15	3.18	3.05	1.0
	CHA	MLB	23	0	0	0	6	0	4¹	5	1	6.2	12.5	6	42%	1.85	4.15	2.40	0.1
Jonathan Stiever	GRF	Rk	21	0	1	0	13	13	28	23	3	2.9	12.5	39	48%	1.14	4.18	3.59	0.8

Much like the estate of Michael Jackson, **Manny Banuelos** gave up a ton of hits this season, before sliding into a bullpen role that led to a sub-3.00 DRA and Triple-A All-Star birth. Who's bad? ⓧ **Aaron Bummer's** funky left-handed sling of a delivery gives him enough movement to crack the Opening Day roster, and the strikeout-to-walk ratio to suggest he should stay there. It also seems to lead to enough command mistakes to push him toward the back of an increasingly long line of young White Sox lefty relievers. ⓧ **Zack Burdi** carried out the family tradition of undergoing Tommy John surgery in late July of 2017, so most of the cabin fever-inducing portions of rehab were over with by the start of the 2018 season. Still, his comeback appearances were not much more than a glorified rehab stint and did not feature his pre-injury, elite velocity. ℗ **Randall Delgado**'s season was weird. He spent the first half continuing his recovery from shoulder and oblique injuries, made seven MLB appearances, was DFA'd, eventually re-signed, got sent to the minors and reappeared in the majors when rosters expanded. His issues, however, remained consistent: an inability to throw strikes and a penchant for giving up homers. ℗ Of the two bespectacled strike-throwers who made their way through the Birmingham Barons rotation in 2018, **Bernardo Flores** is definitely the lesser-known. But while he currently lacks Dane Dunning's mid-rotation starter upside and swing-and-miss stuff, his feel for the changeup is already present and his lanky frame still allows for hope that he could regain his mid-90s college reliever velocity from the left side as he fills out. ℗ Frank Sinatra once sang "Love is lovelier the second time around," which is the first of many hints that he never signed a one-year deal to eat innings with a team that had jettisoned him in an August waiver deal the previous season, only to tear a labrum after three starts. **Miguel Gonzalez**, however, did exactly that. ℗ Getting pushed up a level to clear a path for better prospects is an unusual trigger for a jump forward in performance, but **Jordan Guerrero** surely wouldn't sneeze at any reason to finally be free of Double-A. It's a profile built on a plus changeup and avoiding mistakes, and maybe someday through it the tide will wash him up onto a big league roster for a while. ℗ No one quite knows what baseball in 2020 and beyond will look like, or how well a converted college reliever turned into a low-90s sinkerballer like **Lincoln Henzman** will profile in a big league rotation. But so far, so good, as far as his ability to graze the bottom of bats rather than miss them in A-ball. ℗ As a pure relief prospect who has not yet reached Double-A, there are rules about how excited you're allowed to get about crossfiring young righty **Tyler Johnson**. On the other hand, hachi machi, look at all those whiffs! ℗ The low-90s fastball with a sweeping slider **Jimmy Lambert** of 2017 was not the most interesting prospect. The Jimmy Lambert who now touches 96 mph and pairs it with a hard overhand curveball and a fading changeup is several shades more intriguing, and it'd be polite not to hold it against him for taking his time to arrive at the latter. ℗ Injuries and ineffectiveness have plagued **Evan Marshall**. With the caveat that hard-throwing relievers can randomly unlock success, he's now finished four straight years with ERAs beginning with the numbers 6, 7, 8 and 9. ℗ The Brewers were willing to deal former first-round pick **Kodi Medeiros** because they lost faith in his ability to start, and the White Sox got a glimpse as to why. It's still a good slider, and it still comes out of his left hand, so he should have a career out of the bullpen ahead of him. Maybe it will end up in Milwaukee, given how many White Sox relievers end up there these days. ℗ Last July, FiveThirtyEight published a cheat sheet to help fans determine when to leave a baseball game. ICYMI, it's when **Josh Osich** comes in to pitch. ℗ Sometimes the adage that a college starter can't be judged in his draft year is a cop out, and sometimes they spend the summer leading Mississippi State to the semifinals of the College World Series and get all of 14 scattershot pro innings. **Konnor Pilkington** is a command-over-stuff lefty whose goal will be to slide into the back end of a big league rotation one day, until further evidence is provided. ℗ A six-game September cameo after being plucked from Double-A was never really going to be a clear opportunity for **Jose Ruiz** to distinguish himself beyond "young guy who throws hard." But for a converted catcher in just his third year pitching as a professional, his time in Chicago was more about placing a major league-prorated bow on a season that made the White Sox curious enough to get a look at what they had in their waiver claim gambit. ℗ The universe itself does not revolve around the exploits of college starters in the Pioneer League. But for **Jonathan Stiever**, selected more for athleticism and control than raw stuff, striking out over 30 percent of opposing hitters in his pro debut is a positive development, if not so large as to wield its own gravitational force.

White Sox Prospects

The State of the System:

The prospects have arrived. There's more to come. And yet, and yet... well, this isn't a state of the "organization" I guess. The system is still good.

The Top Ten:

1

Eloy Jimenez   OF   OFP: 70   Likely: 60
ETA: 2019, likely shortly after the clawback date
Born: 11/27/96   Age: 22   Bats: R   Throws: R   Height: 6'4"   Weight: 205
Origin: International Free Agent, 2013

The Report: The only things that could slow Jimenez down in 2018 were minor pectoral and hip injuries. When he was on the field he mashed. While never a hitter that needed to sell out to get his 80-grade raw power into games, the assumption was that Jimenez would start to have the usual power hitter swing-and-miss issues in the upper minors. That did not happen. While it doesn't radically alter the projection—we postulated he could be a plus hitter the last two seasons—it does make us a bit more confident that he'll reach the upper bounds of his OFP. He's not going to win a batting title, but he's shown enough with the bat now to make us think he could win a home run crown.

Jimenez looks like a left fielder at the highest level—and not an asset there—so as we've intoned before, he will have to hit. But the only thing keeping him from proving it in the majors was Chicago's ~~attempts at service time manipulation~~ insistence that he needed further work on his outfield defense. We don't think it's getting all that much better. We also don't think it will matter much in the end.

The Risks: Low. He's hit in the upper minors. The top-of-the-scale raw is making its way into games. He probably should have been up already, but that's now one for the courts to decide, maybe.

Ben Carsley's Fantasy Take: Hey now, this is what ya came for. Jimenez is on the short list of best fantasy prospects in the game. Worst case, Jimenez figures to be a top-25 outfielder in the mold of a modern day Justin Upton who hits 30-plus bombs with a tolerable average. If he really clicks, we could be talking about more of a top-10 outfielder who mashes .280-plus with closer to 40 bombs, a la vintage Nelson Cruz. Either way, you'll be happy you own him for years to come.

2 **Nick Madrigal   IF**   OFP: 70   Likely: 60
ETA: Late 2019 if the White Sox push him. Probably 2020.
Born: 03/05/97   Age: 22   Bats: R   Throws: R   Height: 5'7"   Weight: 165
Origin: Round 1, 2018 Draft (#4 overall)

The Report: If you are reading this blurb, you are the type of high-info fan who doesn't need me to tell you that Nick Madrigal was the best pure hitter in the 2018 draft class. So let's pose a question: Is Nick Madrigal an 8 hit? Granted, the connotation is more "should you give Nick Madrigal an 8 hit?" The scale only works if you use all of it, as KG used to write, but I'm more comfortable giving an 8 OFP than an 8 hit. You can't replicate major-league stuff, scouting, and sequencing in the minors, and you certainly won't do it in the Pac-12.

However, you can see Madrigal's elite barrel control. You might notice he struck out five times in 173 pro plate appearances coming off a full college season where he struck out seven times in 201 PA. It's not a metal bat swing, and there's present 4 raw power here despite his frame. He'll sting baseballs in the gap, and you'd think all that raw would get into play eventually. The White Sox are enthusiastic about moving him to shortstop, and he may have the hands and range for the 6—he's a plus-plus runner—but his arm likely won't allow him to make all the throws you want from a major-league shortstop. A plus second base glove isn't a bad fallback though, nor are "the lesser Altuve seasons" as a reasonable projection. I guess I never really answered the question I asked at the outset, did I?

The Risks: Low. There may not be enough power in the profile to be an impact bat in the end—famous last words nowadays—but Madrigal was the safest bet to hit major-league pitching in his draft class and immediately became one of the safest bets in the minors as well. David Lee likened him to "a major leaguer on rehab" when he saw him in A-ball this summer.

Ben Carsley's Fantasy Take: Aren't you just so, so tired of every short middle infielder getting compared to Dustin Pedroia? I mean, Pedroia isn't even the game's preeminent short middle infielder at this point! It's so annoying. Anyway, uhh, Pedroia hit .305/.372/.457 with an average of 16 bombs and 20 steals per season from 2007-2013. Add a few more steals, and that's likely what we're looking at in Madrigal, who's already got a pretty solid case as a top-15 dynasty league prospect.

3 **Michael Kopech   RHP**   OFP: 70   Likely: 55   ETA: Debuted in 2018
Born: 04/30/96   Age: 23   Bats: R   Throws: R   Height: 6'3"   Weight: 205
Origin: Round 1, 2014 Draft (#33 overall)

The Report: Kopech had another frustrating season, although for slightly different reasons than we're used to with him. At the end of 2017 there was a #narrative that Kopech was taking a little off of his triple-digit fastball to improve his command, prompting speculation that that adjustment explained his dominant second half. Kopech didn't carry it over into 2018 though, and was back to his Wild Thing ways until August, when he posted a 36:1 K:BB ratio and was called up to Chicago.

Then came the torn UCL. 2019 will be a lost season for Kopech, his most frustrating yet. That's all plot, but the story hasn't changed significantly. Kopech still has an elite fastball flanked by a potential plus-plus slider that has led to video game minor league K-rates. His change may actually have gone from "improving" to "improved," although it still isn't a significant part of his repertoire. The problem here is that he's just never showed the ability to throw enough strikes to hit his lofty ceiling for more than one- or two-month bursts. That's better than never doing it at all, but it still leaves us with the same control/command questions on top of the new Tommy John recovery questions. The TJ might accelerate a move to the pen for Kopech, but 18 months can change many things in baseball. For now, all we'll do is bump his risk factor.

The Risks: High. The "not everyone comes back 100% from Tommy John" caveat aside, Kopech does not have much of a track record of throwing enough strikes or enough good strikes to be a front-of-the-rotation starter. Check back in 2020.

Ben Carsley's Fantasy Take: I stood my ground on Kopech last year, holding firm to the notion that he was a top-5 dynasty league pitching prospect even when the going got rough. Unfortunately, there's no real way for me to make that argument now that Kopech is likely 18 months away from any sort of meaningful fantasy contribution. It's still reasonable to hope that Kopech blossoms into a high-WHIP, high-strikeout fantasy starter a la Chris Archer, but there are quite a few red flags at this point. Hold on to him if you've got him, but don't look to aggressively trade for him either.

4 **Dylan Cease   RHP**   OFP: 70   Likely: 55   ETA: Mid-to-late 2019
Born: 12/28/95   Age: 23   Bats: R   Throws: R   Height: 6'2"   Weight: 190
Origin: Round 6, 2014 Draft (#169 overall)

The Report: It feels like we've been waiting a very long time to witness the firepower of this fully armed and operational battle station. After years of caution from both sides of Chi-Town, the White Sox unleashed Cease in the spring, letting him throw full starts on a fairly regular rest cycle. He responded brilliantly, showing off his full arsenal, including an improved slider and change to go along with a fastball and curve combo that both rank among the better pitches in the minors.

The Risks: High—similar to Kopech's, actually. Cease's health record is spotty at best: Tommy John around draft time, some shoulder soreness here, arm fatigue there. His 23 starts and 124 innings in 2018 both represent career-highs, and that's still a good pace off an MLB starter's workload in his fourth full pro season. He might end up being more of a good candidate for the Josh Hader high-leverage multi-inning reliever role than a starter's role, even in a higher-end outcome.

Ben Carsley's Fantasy Take: The Spiderman pointing at himself meme works here with "A healthy Michael Kopech as a dynasty prospect" on one Spidey and "A healthy Dylan Cease as a dynasty prospect" on the other.

5   **Luis Robert**   OF   OFP: 60   Likely: 50
ETA: 2020, give or take a year
Born: 08/03/97   Age: 21   Bats: R   Throws: R   Height: 6'3"   Weight: 185
Origin: International Free Agent, 2017

The Report: The international man of mystery… wasn't really healthy enough to solve much of the mystery, was he? Limited by thumb and knee problems, he never made it out of A-ball and didn't hit much when he was on the field. Sent to the Arizona Fall League to make up for lost reps, he promptly pulled his hamstring. When healthy, he's shown off the high-end speed and hit potential that prompted the White Sox to give him so much money in the first place. Despite uncertainty about the shape of his future performance, there's enough bat speed and control here to give him a real shot to hit for average. He's flashed significant raw power too, but that aspect hasn't quite made it to 7 PM yet. He should comfortably stick in center, perhaps even excelling there.

The Risks: He's a speed guy who keeps hurting his legs. Like last year, we still suspect the underlying tools are there for him to shoot up our lists, but we'll continue to hedge until he puts together a sustained run of health and offensive performance.

Ben Carsley's Fantasy Take: If Robert's injury history prevents him from running a ton or keeps him off the field, obviously that's a big fantasy issue. But people tend to discount just how much rope stealing bases gives a fantasy player: Only 11 players swiped more than 30 bags last season, and only another 17 swiped 20-plus. Let's assume a healthy Robert's floor is something like Ender Inciarte 2018: .265 with 10 bombs and 28 steals with 83 runs scored. That was still enough to qualify as the 21st best outfielder in 5×5 leagues, per ESPN's player rater. Robert is still super valuable, is what we're saying. Be patient.

6   **Dane Dunning**   RHP   OFP: 60   Likely: 50
ETA: Assuming no further arm issues, late 2019.
Born: 12/20/94   Age: 24   Bats: R   Throws: R   Height: 6'4"   Weight: 200
Origin: Round 1, 2016 Draft (#29 overall)

The Report: I'll grouse a lot in these column inches about needing new ways to describe mid-rotation projections. Regardless, Dunning might just be the template for this profile. His body is built to log innings—"eyes of doe and thighs of stallion" as Los Campesinos! sing—with an easy delivery and relatively compact arm action that portends at least average command of four at least average pitches. His fastball is a low-90s heavy sinker with wicked armside run. Dunning spots it to both sides, and when he's locating well armside he might as well be playing catch. The movement and command make the velocity play up, and you could call it a potential plus fastball without raising my hackles.

The secondaries all settle in between average and solid-average. Dunning offers two different breaking ball looks: An 11-5 big breaking curve that shows a bit early, but that he commands well, and a shorter mid-80s slider that almost looks cutterish at times. His feel for the change can come and go, but it flashes plus with good sink and fade when he gets it in to lefties. There's no clear major-league bat misser, but everything works, and everything works well off each other. Everything was humming along for Dunning in 2018, and he might have even seen big-league time in September if not for a sprained elbow that put him on the shelf for the entire second half of the season. Pitchers, man.

The Risks: Medium. Dunning is throwing again with no issues, but "elbow sprain" is always going to make me dramatically tug at my collar in a Vaudevillian way. Beyond that, this profile is carried at least in part by pitch mix and command, and that doesn't always get fully sussed out until major-league bats get involved.

Ben Carsley's Fantasy Take: Dunning has proximity on his side, but upside and that elbow sprain are two pretty big strikes against him. Do I prefer him to many of the other dozen-plus mid-rotation starters who could be pitching by July? Yes. Does that make him a lock for the top-101? No, but if he misses it won't be by much.

7 **Luis Alexander Basabe OF**   OFP: 50   Likely: 40   ETA: 2020
Born: 08/26/96 Age: 22 Bats: B Throws: R Height: 6'0" Weight: 160
Origin: International Free Agent, 2012

The Report: Basabe began 2018 where he ended 2017, in High-A Winston-Salem. In his first go-around, the athletic outfielder didn't display much power and scuffled through an injury-laden campaign that finally ended when he got surgery to repair his left meniscus. 2018 was a different story, as a healthy Basabe looked more comfortable and showed a much better approach.

At the plate, Basabe uses a moderate leg kick to create plenty of torque from his lower half, and that's something that just wasn't there the year before. It's a sweet pull-happy swing from the left side, and there's above-average raw power in the bat from that side of the dish. He was listed at just 160 pounds last year, so he has room to add weight.

Basabe's ultimate value will be shaped by his defensive home, and I'm fairly optimistic he'll be able to stick in center. He tracks the ball well and takes a good first step, though his routes could use a little work. The arm is above-average and would play up in a corner spot, but he'll have every opportunity to make it work in center. While he didn't have the same kind of offensive performance in Double-A as he did in Winston-Salem, he looked healthy again and it was a positive season overall.

The Risks: High. The swing can get a little long, with a mild bat wrap that sometimes hinders his ability to get the stick through the zone. If he can't play center, he loses value and perhaps winds up in a reserve role.

Ben Carsley's Fantasy Take: Basabe is a better IRL prospect than a fantasy one, but he's not without his uses in our world. The hope is he ends up as a solid all-around contributor and fantasy OF4/5 once he grows into a little more power. The fear is that he becomes the type of generic 20-homer threat who's only interesting if he's playing every day. Still, if you held on to him after his miserable 2017, his stock is trending up.

Blake Rutherford   OF   OFP: 50   Likely: 40   ETA: Late 2020
Born: 05/02/97   Age: 22   Bats: L   Throws: R   Height: 6'3"   Weight: 195
Origin: Round 1, 2016 Draft (#18 overall)

The Report: Rutherford makes fairly consistent contact from the left side of the plate, with quick hands and a fluid swing without a lot of pre-pitch noise. He's always had an advanced feel at the plate, and he's able to get ahead in counts and drive the ball into the gaps. For now, power isn't a huge part of his game. He's still young and still learning his body, and you'd naturally expect him to add some weight as he matures. If he can incorporate more lift in the swing it would be easier to project him as a future 20-homer guy.

It's also worth mentioning that Rutherford has struggled with southpaws throughout his minor league career. While he saw time at all three outfield spots last season, the majority of it was in right field. A corner spot may suit him best, as his average arm and solid-average speed are perhaps a bit short of requirements in center, particularly if he gets bigger.

The Risks: High. As Rutherford grows into his body, he's less likely to stay in center. Could a team put him there? Sure. But he's going to be better suited as a corner outfielder, and if his power doesn't develop, he's going to be a tweener. Factor in the concerns against left-handed pitching, and there are an awful lot of variables in the profile.

Ben Carsley's Fantasy Take: Basically you're hoping for Stephen Piscotty as a best-case outcome here. That gives Rutherford a pretty modest ceiling, but I like his odds of hitting it more than most. A potential very back-end of the top-101 guy for me, though it's likely he falls short in favor of higher upside dudes. Still, if you held on for his rough 2017 second-half, good job.

9

Alec Hansen RHP   OFP: 50   Likely: 40
ETA: Over/under is around early-2020.
Born: 10/10/94   Age: 24   Bats: R   Throws: R   Height: 6'7"   Weight: 235
Origin: Round 2, 2016 Draft (#49 overall)

The Report: Oof. There's a player development maxim that once a player shows a particular ability, he can always rediscover it. This might run the other way for Hansen, in that his 2016 implosion in college shows that it can all fall apart for him at any time. Hansen came down with the dreaded forearm tightness in spring training, didn't show up on a field until June, and was beyond terrible upon his return. He struggled mightily to throw strikes, and after consecutive starts of six, nine, and seven walks in Double-A, he was demoted back to High-A. He wasn't much better there, failing to make it to the fifth inning in any of his five starts and walking more than he struck out. We're still ranking him because there's still a big fastball and breaking ball kicking around somewhere in there, and he has an injury excuse. But he's gotta get back on track.

The Risks: Extreme. Well, if he keeps on the present track with the whole balls and strikes thing he's never going to reach the majors. Forearm stuff generally isn't great for a pitcher. There was lots of reliever risk here anyway, and it would not surprise me at all if he gets it together in the pen and even becomes dominant, a la Dellin Betances. Both the positive and negative risk probably aren't quite captured in the OFP/likely scale.

Ben Carsley's Fantasy Take: I'd rather roll the dice on someone like Hansen than on any of the myriad back-end starter types who appear at this junction on lists for lesser farm systems. That's a bit of a false choice though, and while Hansen should be owned if your league rosters 150-plus prospects, he's really just a lottery ticket. For our purposes, his best odds at sustained success may come as a closer.

10

Micker Adolfo OF   OFP: 50   Likely: 40   ETA: 2021
Born: 09/11/96   Age: 22   Bats: R   Throws: R   Height: 6'3"   Weight: 200
Origin: International Free Agent, 2013

The Report: Adolfo's injury log is staggeringly long for a 22-year-old position player. Ankle and hand issues bothered him in 2015 and 2016, and then his 2017 was cut short after he punched a wall and fractured his hand. Last year, he labored through a torn flexor muscle and strained UCL until July, when the White Sox shut him down so he could undergo Tommy John surgery. His 2018 maladies kept him away from the outfield and limited him to DH duties.

Adolfo has plus raw power, and between the loft in the swing and his considerable upper-body strength, he gets to it pretty often in games. He doesn't have a great feel for contact and there will be some swing and miss in his game, but his eye is improving and he's chasing fewer pitches out of the zone these days. He'll have to continue to make adjustments to pick up off-speed stuff, but damn it, he'll hit mistakes and he's got a cannon for an arm; there are usable tools in the shed.

The Risks: Very High. The injury bug has bit Adolfo in some way in each of the last four years. While he finished the year at High-A, he's also going to be 23 in September of 2019, so you'd like to see some sort of progress next season. It's unclear when he'll be ready to return from Tommy John, but when he does, he needs to stay in the lineup.

Ben Carsley's Fantasy Take: He could be interesting if he ends up getting regular playing time, but that's a pretty big if at this point. Frankly, it's not too difficult to find guys like this on the waiver wire even in super deep leagues. You can pass.

The Next Six:

Zack Collins   C
Born: 02/06/95   Age: 24   Bats: L   Throws: R   Height: 6'3"   Weight: 220
Origin: Round 1, 2016 Draft (#10 overall)

I got a chat question this summer about Collins 2018 season so far, and described it as "holding serve." The combination of his long, leveraged swing and good eye at the plate has kept him on the three true outcome slugger path, which would make him an easy top ten guy in this system if we thought he was even passable at catcher. But Collins still struggles with his receiving and spent a significant amount of time in Birmingham as a DH (FWIW, our advanced catching metrics had him as one of the worst framers in Double-A). Collins has a strong arm, but there is a lot of bulk to get going, and his throwing mechanics aren't always clean. Teams are far less willing to play this type of profile behind the plate these days, and it's possible that Collins just isn't playable in the majors as a backstop. The bat won't be quite good enough to carry first base, so while strictly speaking he's a 5/4 type profile, the actual variance here is much larger.

Luis Gonzalez   OF
Born: 09/10/95   Age: 23   Bats: L   Throws: L   Height: 6'1"   Weight: 185
Origin: Round 3, 2017 Draft (#87 overall)

Gonzalez has perceived makeup concerns—which may partially explain why he fell to the third round in the 2017 draft—but his on-field performance in 2018 offers little to quibble with. He has one of those sweet lefty swings and hits line drives line to line. There's enough loft in the swing to project average game pop, and Gonzalez stays in well against lefties. He's splitting time between center and the corners at present, and to be honest he doesn't exactly have a lower half that screams "up the middle" player. Gonzalez also mashed at levels you'd expect a college bat to mash at. The offensive profile still may be good enough to carry an everyday corner outfield spot, but we'll know more when the polished New Mexico product gets his first taste of Double-A next season.

 Ian Hamilton   RHP
Born: 06/16/95   Age: 24   Bats: R   Throws: R   Height: 6'0"   Weight: 200
Origin: Round 11, 2016 Draft (#326 overall)

 Ryan Burr   RHP
Born: 05/28/94   Age: 25   Bats: R   Throws: R   Height: 6'4"   Weight: 225
Origin: Round 5, 2015 Draft (#136 overall)

HAMILTON: Pardon me, are you relief pitcher Ryan Burr, sir?

I'm Ian Hamilton, flamethrowing reliever at your service, sir

God, I wish we put up more WAR

Then we could prove we're worth more than we're collectively bargained for

BURR: Fastball less, slider more

Okay, so usually I run out of ways to describe fastball/slider college closers much later in the offseason. Hamilton is the slightly harder-throwing one, and Burr is the taller one. They're close friends and remarkably similar prospects on the whole. Both blew us all away in Double-A and Triple-A this year, and both came up in August and struggled a bit in the majors. Usual caveats about command and functionality of third pitch from this profile also apply if they're going to stay in the room where it happens. The Hahn administration has built a lot of potential high-end reliever stock, so it remains to be seen whether the White Sox bullpen is wide enough for both. And yes, they're in on the joke.

 Jake Burger   3B
Born: 04/10/96   Age: 23   Bats: R   Throws: R   Height: 6'2"   Weight: 210
Origin: Round 1, 2017 Draft (#11 overall)

The Double Stack took a double thwack to his 2018 season. Two Achilles ruptures, the first in spring training, the second while rehabbing, cost him an entire year of development. Burger was already a large adult son—check that nickname again—and likely bound for the cold corner in the medium term, but the injuries will certainly accelerate that process. There's enough uncertainty in his pro career in general now that you could argue for dropping him off the list entirely, but... well, we really like the bat.

 Seby Zavala   C
Born: 08/28/93   Age: 25   Bats: R   Throws: R   Height: 5'11"   Weight: 215
Origin: Round 12, 2015 Draft (#352 overall)

While BP's website wants to autocorrect this guy's name to "Sexy Zavala," there is nothing in the profile here that suggests such nominative determinism. Zavala is... well, "Zack-Collins-lite" isn't precisely correct. He's a superior defender to Collins—one of the reasons he was bumped to the International League first—but not so good that you'd want him as your first choice backstop. The bat isn't quite as loud as Collins, and backup backstops nowadays don't fit the "medium-power, fringy glove" profile that was all the rage in the 2000s; where have you gone, Henry Blanco? Zavala also isn't athletic enough to be a "jack-of-all-trades-and-also-a-catcher," which is en vogue on the north side of town. So we're left with a bit of a square peg prospect, although at a quick glance he might appear like many of the fringy catching prospects in most teams' 11-20.

Others of note:

Bernardo Flores, LHP, Double-A Birmingham

Flores is an uptempo southpaw with a high leg kick and hand break that sends his lean limbs in a bunch of different directions. It looks gangly but it's deceptive, he repeats well, and there isn't pronounced effort at any point. His fastball only sits low-90s, but Flores puts it where he wants and can change eye levels effectively. As you might have deduced from the lead-in, the changeup has above-average projection. He sells it well and can get it in to righties with sink and fade. He has two breaking balls—a slow, inconsistent curve that rolls across the plate and a slurvy slider—and both are below average. Flores doesn't really have a consistent bat-missing option, but there's enough command and change he could soak up some innings as a 5th starter/swingman/middle reliever.

Gavin Sheets, 1B, Advanced-A Winston Salem

Last year Sheets clocked in the Next Ten as a college first baseman with plus raw, not much of a pro track record, and a positional future that would put a lot of pressure on the bat. These are almost as common as polished lefties with an above-average change. As much as we love Big Boy SZN here at the BP Prospect Team, it's not as aesthetically pleasing as those crafty lefties, and in 2018 Sheets couldn't even offer much in the way of majestic dingers. Despite a leveraged swing and only average bat speed, he also didn't strike out all that much. He did, however, take 52 walks. Given his pedigree, he should have smashed the Carolina League, but after a weird season, for now we can just say there is still a lot of pressure on the bat.

Zack Burdi, RHP, complex-league AZL

Burdi has fallen behind the other power relief arms in the White Sox org while he sat on the sidelines rehabbing his 2017 Tommy John surgery. But there is a reason he went in the first round as a relief-only college arm. Burdi offers triple-digit heat, a wipeout slider, and he was essentially major-league-ready when his

UCL blew. His few weeks of rehab in the AZL were uneven, as you'd expect, and he's getting some extra reps in Fall Ball as well. We'll have to wait to see him in camp next spring before confirming the closer stuff is still there, but if so he could walk into the White Sox Opening Day bullpen. Yep, that's all I got. I've never seen Hamilton.

Top Talents 25 and Under (born 4/1/93 or later):

1. Eloy Jimenez
2. Tim Anderson
3. Yoan Moncada
4. Nick Madrigal
5. Michael Kopech
6. Dylan Cease
7. Luis Robert
8. Reynaldo Lopez
9. Dane Dunning
10. Luis Alexander Basabe

The top three are already major league contributors or very close to it. Jimenez's superstar potential far outweighs the already productive if not quite finished products that are Anderson and Moncada.

Anderson over Moncada was a tough call, but the placement says more about the strides the former made in 2018 than the latter's perceived struggles. Anderson's essentially league-average offense in 2017 made him... well, essentially a league-average player, especially given how well his glove has come along at short. He paired a sterling defensive season with essentially the same offensive production as ever, albeit with a considerable leap in the power department. As a sure-handed defender at a key position with adequate offense and solid power, he gets the edge.

Moncada hasn't yet matured into the type of player many expected when he was a top prospect. Still, his league-leading strikeout total obscures some growth at the plate, particularly in eschewing pitches outside of the strike zone (18th best among qualified hitters). Even with his contact issues last year, he still showed enough of the tools people once raved about to portend a career as a very good regular, even if he doesn't look like a superstar.

Kopech likely would have ranked No. 2 on this list if he hadn't torn his UCL, which will keep him out until 2020. He slots in right behind Madrigal, the White Sox top pick in the 2018 draft. Madrigal more than held his own in High-A in the few months we saw of him following the draft. Kopech still has the higher ceiling, but arm injuries to pitchers are... well, you know.

The back five falls right in line with the prospect rankings above, with Lopez sandwiched in the middle. Lopez was just about the only young White Sox pitcher to not suffer any significant setback in 2018. He outpitched his peripherals for most of the season and showed enough durability to suggest he can stick in the rotation. He likely settles in as something of a backend starter, which limits his ceiling to the point where I'm comfortable putting talented but volatile prospects like Cease and Robert ahead of him. Still, his raw stuff—even if it winds up in the bullpen—is good enough to outweigh the high floor/low ceiling types like Dunning (who also missed time with an injury) and Basabe.

Part 3: Featured Articles

The Hole in The Shift is Fixing Itself

Russell Carleton

I've been on a bit of a mission against The Shift of late. I'm not out to get The Shift for the usual reasons that people oppose it. The words "the right way to play the game" won't be found on my lips. If a team wants to pursue a strategy that is within the rules and it works, then by all means, they have my blessing (not that they need it). Instead, my concern with The Shift is a worry that it doesn't work, or at least that it has a flaw that needs fixing.

The data show that while The Shift does a decent job of preventing singles on balls in play (what it's supposed to do), it also increases the number of walks that happen in front of it, and the number of additional walks outweighs the number of singles saved. It's a problem because you can't throw a guy out if he gets to walk to first base.

But the "why" was important. It seemed that The Shift was changing the way in which pitchers pitched. We saw that there were fewer fastballs thrown in front of The Shift than we might otherwise expect, and that pitchers tended to stay out of the strike zone a little more. Not by a lot. In fact, it might not even be visible to the naked eye. The percentage of pitches that are out of the zone goes from 51.0 to 53.3 from a standard defense (two right/two left) to a full shift (three on one side). That difference stands up even after we control for the types of hitters that get shifted against. And it's enough to drive up the walk rate to where it cancels out the benefits that teams thought they were getting with The Shift... and then some.

But there was some hope. I found that when individual pitchers stayed closer to the in-zone/out-of-zone mix that they used without The Shift on, they could still get the benefits of The Shift without the walk problems. So, in theory, a team could simply figure out a way to convince its pitchers to not fall prey to the walk trap and The Shift would once again be their friend.

It's reasonable to think that some teams might be more hip to this idea than others. Maybe some figured it out a year before the others. Maybe they were better at getting the message across to their pitchers. Or, maybe no one has figured it out yet.

Warning! Gory Mathematical Details Ahead!

I used data from 2015-2017, made available through MLB's data portal, Baseball Savant. They are kind enough to note when teams are using an infield shift (three fielders on one side of second base), as opposed to a "strategic shift" (someone's playing a bit out of position, but it's not quite that drastic) or a "standard" alignment.

Since we're doing this by team, I can't just look at raw walk rates, because we know that some teams have good pitchers and others have not-so-good pitchers. Some have a mix of both. I used the log-odds ratio method to take into account a batter's general walking proclivities, and a pitcher's as well, and then shoving them into a binary logistic regression. Then, I asked the computer to generate a specific coefficient for each team's pitchers, for when they went into The Shift and how that affected their walk rate.

Using those coefficients, I was able to project what would happen if a league-average pitcher faced a league-average hitter (which we expect would product a league-average walk rate; from 2015-2017, 7.7 percent of plate appearances ended in a walk) and then just switched his hat. Here's the top five and the bottom five:

Top 5 Teams	Projected Shift Walk Rate	Bottom 5 Teams	Projected Shift Walk Rate
Rockies	6.2%	Rangers	11.2%
Pirates	6.7%	Mets	10.4%
Indians	7.2%	Dodgers	10.2%
Astros	7.3%	Cardinals	9.9%
Braves	7.7%	Tigers	9.7%

There are probably people out there right now trying to figure out what the common thread is among the top and bottom teams. I'm sure, because this is Baseball Prospectus, people are already trying to make the case that sabermetric "early adopters" have some sort of edge here. I think that the more interesting piece is that by the time you get to fifth place in The Shift, we're at league average.

As a sanity check, I examined the issue on a pitch-by-pitch level, looking at how often pitchers threw their pitches in the GameDay strike zone, and again using the same basic methodology and getting team-specific coefficients. The names on the list re-arranged themselves, but the idea was the same, and the two lists correlated with an R of .593.

There's a reason that I don't usually do this type of leaderboard post. I don't really know what the Rockies, Pirates, Indians, Astros, and Braves have in common, or what they have that the bottom five don't. I can put a shrug emoji here and say, "Well, it must be something!" but that seems like a cop-out. Instead, I'd like to present another table and suggest that the table above doesn't even really matter anymore.

Year	League Percent Outside K Zone (Full Shift)	League Percent in K Zone (No Shift)	Difference
2015	54.1%	51.1%	3.0%
2016	53.3%	50.9%	2.4%
2017	52.6%	50.9%	1.7%
2018	52.0%	50.7%	1.3%

The hole in The Shift is fixing itself, and it's coming down really fast league wide. In my earlier work on The Shift, I suggested that until teams stopped having such a huge difference between their out-of-zone rate with and without The Shift on, there would just be too many walks for The Shift to make sense. It seems that all 30 of them have been working toward just that. I once estimated that it takes about 10 years for an idea to filter its way through baseball. At this rate, it looks like teams are going to catch up a lot faster than that. And yeah, they're all saber-smart now.

It's likely that whatever magic it was that the Rockies and Pirates had has made its way to Texas and Queens. Or is at least on its way. And if teams are committing to fixing the walk problem, then it's likely that they will continue shifting and shifting a lot.

And eventually it's going to actually make sense for them to do it.

—Russell Carleton is a former author of Baseball Prospectus and now an analyst for the New York Mets.

The State of the Quality Start

Rob Mains

One of the seven things you (probably) didn't know about the 2018 season is that quality starts—defined as a start lasting six or more innings with three or fewer earned runs allowed—as a percentage of total starts cratered to an all-time low of 41 percent. I want to look a little more deeply into this, since it's been a while (May of 2016, to be exact) since I've examined quality starts.

The term *quality start* is credited to *Philadelphia Inquirer* sportswriter John Lowe. It's been derided ever since he coined it in December of 1985. Three runs in six innings? That's a 4.50 ERA! In what world is that a measure of quality?

Let's start with that criticism. It's true that 3 x 9 / 6 = 4.5. (You came here for this sort of high-level math, right?) But it's also true that type of start, meeting the bare minimum for earning a quality start, is unusual. Here's the proportion of quality starts in which the pitcher lasted exactly six innings and yielded exactly three earned runs. (I'm going to confine this analysis to the 30-team era, 1998-present. Almost all data retrieved in this article is via the Baseball-Reference Play Index.)

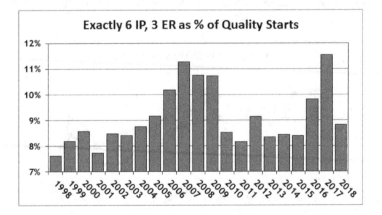

There were 1,997 quality starts in 2018. Only 176, or fewer than one in 11, featured a pitcher going six innings and allowing three earned runs. Put another way, the percentage of quality starts that resulted in a 4.50 ERA (8.8 percent) is less than half the percentage of games in which a batter hit two home runs and his team lost (22.5 percent; 237-69 won-lost). That doesn't impugn hitting two homers.

So if a 4.50 ERA isn't the norm, what is? How good are quality starts?

Pretty good, it turns out. First, on a team level:

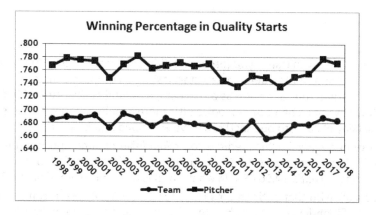

Teams receiving a quality start from their pitcher won 68.4 percent of their games in 2018, in line with the 30-team era average of 67.9 percent. A team with a .684 winning percentage wins 111 games. Getting a quality start is definitely a good thing. Individual pitchers throwing quality starts have a higher winning percentage because a big slice of team losses is assigned to a reliever.

If teams do well in quality starts, how well do the starting pitchers do? Again, very well.

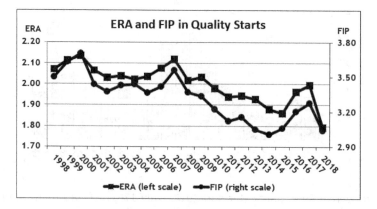

Pitchers in quality starts had a 1.79 ERA (blue line) in 2018, *the lowest in the 30-team era*. Their FIP was higher, 3.04, but still excellent. In the 30-team era, only 2014 had a lower FIP for quality starts, 3.01.

But, of course, the run environment in 2014 was different. Teams in 2014 scored 4.07 runs per game, the fewest in a non-strike year since 1976. They scored 4.45 runs per game in 2018. So surrendering a 3.04 FIP in 2018 is more impressive than 3.01 in 2014. Accordingly, let's look at ERA and FIP in quality starts relative to league averages.

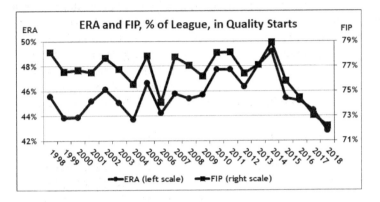

This tells a more dramatic story. Starting pitchers in 2018 gave up a 4.19 ERA and a 4.21 FIP. Starters in quality starts gave up a 1.79 ERA, 43 percent of the league average. Starters in quality starts gave up a 3.04 FIP, 72 percent of the league average. Both of these marks represent lows in the 30-team era.

The takeaway here is this: *Quality starts are better, relative to other starts, than they've ever been over the past 21 years.*

Maybe during the winter I'll look at this over a longer arc of time. For now, though, we can definitively say quality starts are the best they've ever been since the Diamondbacks and Rays joined the majors.

Yet, paradoxically, they're down.

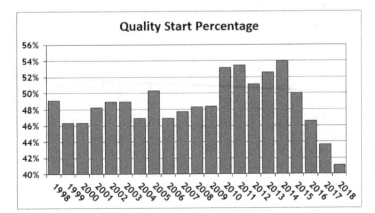

This graph covers only the 30-team era. In my article last week, though, I looked at the years 1908-2018. The result was the same. The 41 percent of starts in 2018 that were quality starts are an all-time low, well below the runners-up: 1930's 43 percent (the year teams scored an all-time record 5.55 runs per game) and last year's 44 percent.

The normal explanation for a dip in quality start percentage is an increase in scoring. When teams score a lot of runs, it's harder for starting pitchers to last six or more innings and limit opponents to three earned runs. From 1998 to 2014, the correlation between runs scored per game and the percentage of starts that were quality starts was -0.94. That means there was an extremely close relationship: More runs, fewer quality starts. Too small a sample? Go back to the start of the Expansion Era, 1961, and the relationship is even more negative, a -0.95 correlation, though 2014.

But that's broken down over the past four years:

- 2015: Runs per game increased from 4.07 to 4.25, quality start percentage decreased from 54.0 to 50.1. Yes, that's a negative relationship, but the regression model would predict a decline of 1.5 percentage points. We got 3.9 instead.

- 2016: Runs per game increased from 4.25 to 4.48, quality start percentage decreased from 50.1 to 46.6. Past experience would suggest a decline of just 1.8 percentage points. We got 3.4.

- 2017: Runs per game increased from 4.48 to 4.65, quality start percentage decreased from 46.6 to 43.6. Again, the direction's right, but the magnitude isn't. Using the relationship from 1998 to 2014, that increase in scoring should've reduced quality starts by 1.3 percentage points, not 2.9.

- 2018: Runs per game declined from 4.65 to 4.45. That should've resulted in the quality start percentage moving in the other direction, rising 1.6 points. It didn't. It fell 2.6 points, as noted, to an all-time low.

Granted, we're talking about just four years here. Maybe they're outliers. But I don't think they are. Quality starts, as noted, are as good or better than ever. But they're rarer than ever as well. And I think I know why.

To get a quality start, you need to allow three or fewer earned and pitch at least six innings. That's 18 outs. Here's a graph showing the number of starting pitchers who limited their opponents to three or fewer earned runs but got pulled after pitching at least five innings but fewer than six:

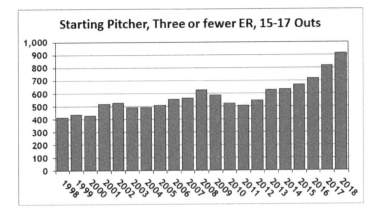

A pitcher getting 15 outs pitched five innings. A pitcher getting 16 outs pitched 5 1/3. A pitcher getting 17 outs pitched 5 2/3. More than ever before, pitchers are being removed from games in which they are within 1-3 outs of a quality start, falling just short of the six-inning finish line. Widespread acknowledgement of the times-through-the-order penalty and a flotilla of available bullpen arms is making the quality start simultaneously both more excellent and more rare.

Which is ironic, given that we saw a new post-war quality start record this season:

Rank	Pitcher	Season	Consecutive QS
1	Jacob deGrom	2018	24
2	Bob Gibson	1968	22
-	Chris Carpenter	2005	22
4	Johan Santana	2004	21
5	Luis Tiant	1968	20
-	Mike Scott	1986	20
-	Jake Arrieta	2015	20
8	Robin Roberts	1952	19
-	Tom Seaver	1973	19
-	Jack Morris	1983	19
-	Greg Maddux	1998	19
-	Josh Johnson	2010	19
-	Jon Lester	2014	19

While there have been longer streaks spread over multiple seasons, no pitcher since World War II threw more consecutive quality starts in one year than Jacob deGrom this year. The fact that he did in a year in which quality starts were the rarest they've ever been adds to the accomplishment. ▨

—*Rob Mains is an author of Baseball Prospectus.*

Heads-Up Hacking—The First Pitch

Matthew Trueblood

Batters fell behind in a higher percentage of all plate appearances in 2018 than in any previous season for which we have pitch-by-pitch data. That kind of granular information goes back only to 1988, but we might safely assume (given all we know about baseball as it had been before that, and as it has been in the years since) that batters have *never* fallen behind at a higher rate than they did last season.

Through the 1990s, the percentage of all plate appearances that began 0-1 hovered in the high 30s and low 40s. In the 2000s, it rose steadily but slowly, through the mid-40s. In 2018, 49.8 percent of all trips to the plate began 0-1. That, as much as anything, captures in microcosm the nature of hitting in MLB today.

A countdown clock toward strike three begins ticking almost the moment a batter takes his place in the box. The league's adjusted OPS+ on the first pitch was higher in 2018 than ever before, and that has been true in most of the last 10 seasons. Batters hit .264/.289/.442 in all plate appearances in which they swung at the first pitch last season, and .241/.330/.395 in all plate appearances in which they took that first offering.

The percentage differences in batting average and isolated power there favor swinging at the first pitch by more than in any season since 1988, while the difference in on-base percentage favors taking by more than ever. If you want to get on base at a decent clip, it's a good idea to be patient, but you run the risk of missing the only chances you'll get to produce power.

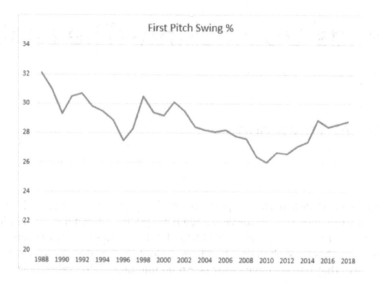

The league swung at the first pitch 28.8 percent of the time in 2018. With the isolated exception of 2015, that's the highest that number has climbed since 2002, but it might not be high enough. With the help of BP research maven Rob McQuown, I looked at the aggregate Called Strike Probability (CSProb) on the first pitch for each season since 2008, when the implementation of PITCHf/x first made measuring that possible. It's risen sharply during that period.

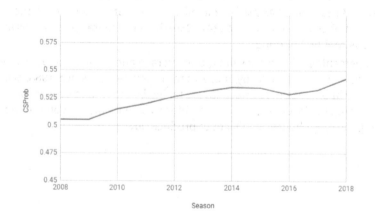

Called Strike Probability, First Pitch of PA (2008-2018)

Called Strike Probability is exactly what it sounds like: a pitch with a given CSProb has roughly that chance of being called a strike, if not swung at. In 2018, a batter who took 100 first pitches from a random sampling of the league's pitchers might expect to fall behind 54 or 55 times—up from 50 or 51 times in 2008. Almost regardless of pitch type (and, notably, especially in the case of fastballs), the first pitch tends to have more of the zone right now than ever before.

Pitchers are better at throwing strikes. They have better stuff, and believe more in their ability to miss bats within the zone. Perhaps most importantly, they know that batters are looking for one thing on the first pitch: a fastball. If they don't get it, they're likely to take the pitch. Check out how the use of sinkers and four-seamers on the first pitch has changed in a decade:

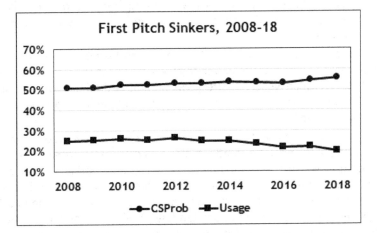

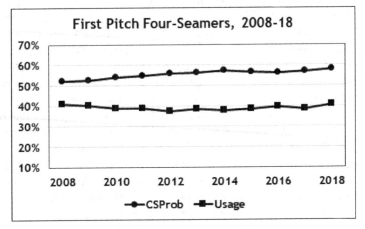

The sinker is losing its place in baseball, but the rate at which pitchers have thrown it on the first pitch hasn't dropped any faster than its usage rate in other counts. Pitchers have actually gone to their four-seamer *more* often to open counts, in the last few years, after a dip in the 2012-2015 period. What's really changed, though, and what shows up in both charts above, is that pitchers are catching more of the zone with first-pitch fastballs than they were a decade ago, or a half-decade ago. They're attacking right away, even with the pitch they know batters are expecting. The message is pretty clear: batters are being too passive.

Sliders, curves, and changeups each have more of the zone when thrown on the first pitch than they did several years ago, too, though the effect is less pronounced. Pitchers have seen the numbers; they know batters are doing better on the first pitch itself. They still feel safe throwing more and better strikes than ever before, figuring they'll come out ahead as long as they keep getting ahead to open each battle.

The Moneyball revolution brought an increased league-wide focus on OBP, which resulted in a de facto mandate to take a more patient tack at the plate. It worked very well for a while, as batters with poor plate discipline were compelled to either adjust or be expelled from the league, and pitchers with poor control were slowly weeded out.

However, concurrent with that revolution, and spurred by it in some ways, was the evolution of the pitching paradigm that now dominates the game. As batters ratcheted up their focus on inflating pitch counts and working walks, pitchers honed theirs on throwing strikes and missing bats. The league's understanding of what makes a good pitcher improved at least as much, from the mid-1990s through the mid-2000s, as its understanding of what makes a good hitter. As amphetamines and other performance-enhancing drugs were phased mostly out of the game, and as PITCHf/x broke onto the scene, individuals and teams learned how to exploit the evolved approaches of even the smartest hitters.

The ability to avoid making outs is still the most valuable one in baseball, but the magnitude of its eclipse of slugging is smaller than ever. To a greater extent than power, on-base skills derive their value from chaining—from the on-base skill levels of the players on either side of a given individual. Eleven years ago, when the housing crisis hit, people learned the hard way that the value of their homes depended a good deal on the values of their neighbors' homes. The same wasn't true, though, of their cars. So it is now, with OBP and SLG.

The global OBP in 2018 was .318. The only seasons since the Dead Ball Era in which the league got on base at a worse clip were 2013-2015, 1988, 1971-1972, and 1963-1968. This is all happening despite the aforementioned evolution of the science of hitting. It's happening despite a shift in approach and focus, one that would steer OBP ever higher, if only it were working.

Instead, it's sitting at a low ebb, and while it does so, even guys who get on base often are a little less helpful than they were 10 years ago—or 20, or 40, or 60, or 70, or 80, or 90. They're less helpful, that is, because unless there happen to be three or four other guys in the lineup who get on just as regularly, their contribution is merely to forestall the inevitable. Runs happen, increasingly, when a sudden bang happens, and that means attacking early in the count—because pitchers are sure as hell doing that.

In a league making contact on barely 75 percent of its swings, and a league in which an increasing number of pitchers can throw multiple off-speed pitches for strikes in any count, the only way to consistently generate offense is going to be aggressive. This isn't necessarily true for individuals, like Mookie Betts and Jose Ramirez, who make a lot of contact and have excellent plate discipline, and whose power comes from such natural quickness in a short stroke. Most players have to make tradeoffs, though, whether it be lowering their contact rate or raising their chase rate, in order to consistently make the quality of contact necessary to survive in today's game.

Highest %	Lowest %
Javier Baez – 48.3	Joe Mauer – 4.6
Freddie Freeman – 47.1	Mookie Betts – 9.7
Ozzie Albies – 46.3	Brett Gardner – 10.7
Jose Altuve – 44.2	Jose Ramirez – 12.0
Nick Castellanos – 44.1	Jason Kipnis – 13.8
Joey Gallo – 42.3	Jesus Aguilar – 14.5
Corey Dickerson – 40.9	Xander Bogaerts – 15.8
Salvador Perez – 40.8	Brian Dozier – 16.3
Eddie Rosario – 40.7	Mike Trout – 17.6
Nick Ahmed – 40.4	Yasmani Grandal – 17.6

Top 10 and Bottom 10 Hitters, First-Pitch Swing Rate (2018)

The question isn't which of these lists one prefers, but what they each convey, qualitatively, about the cat-and-mouse game of early-count hitting. Those top five on the left, especially, drive home the fact that for most players, getting aggressive early in the count is now key to keeping strikeout rate down and hitting for power.

For now, the message is: pitchers are coming right after batters with the nastiest stuff they've ever had. Batters had better stop giving away strike one and force hurlers to adjust, or the global OBP crisis is only going to get worse. ▪

—Matthew Trueblood is an author of Baseball Prospectus.

A Hymn for the Index Stat

Patrick Dubuque

We survived without computers. I know this, because I remember the day when my dad hooked up his brand-new Atari 400 computer to the back of our 12-inch Magnavox television, and the perfect blue of the memo pad lit up for the first time. I was born just on the edge of that transitional generation, of learning cursive and balancing checkbooks and just doing math all the time, constant manual arithmetic.

It still amazes me. We learned how to sail ships without computers. We learned how to do calculus. We built towers that didn't fall down, most of the time. We engineered catapults to knock them down anyway. We built a robust system of philosophy called "utilitarianism," founded on the principle that the good of an action is evaluated by summing the effects of that action, which is the kind of formula that would make the world's mainframes crash. The whole foundation of statistics as a field is "here's math you could easily do but would die of old age first."

The fact of the matter is that there is too much math in the world to do. There are too many things changing, and too many things too small to notice, for us to handle. At some point, they become too much for the computers to handle as well, which is why we have chaos theory and undetectable earthquakes, but it's not an even fight. At some point, we fall back on intuition, and given how under-equipped we are, we're forced to bestow that intuition with some sort of supernatural superiority, the "gut feeling," that we can't prove because we can only intuit that our intuition is better.

We're all lousy at intuition, and wonderful at lying to ourselves about it. The honest truth is that computers are far better at intuition than we are, because in order to know what feels "off" you have to know what's "on." In order to do that you have to constantly reassess the average of everything, then re-rank your own experience against it.

Test your own, by comparing these three anonymous lines:

Player	G	HR	AVG	OBP	SLG
Player A	156	38	.259	.342	.535
Player B	154	38	.280	.348	.527
Player C	158	38	.266	.343	.509

These all seem like pretty similar players, right? The second one a touch more batted-ball dependent, the third a little less strong, but all pretty good hitters. And you'd be right, about the latter. Not the former.

Here's the breakdown:

- Player A: 1991 Howard Johnson, 141 DRC+
- Player B: 1996 Dean Palmer, 121 DRC+
- Player C: 2018 Giancarlo Stanton, 114 DRC+

Baseball is fortunate to have escaped the seismic shifts of so many other sports, where the talents and performances of other eras are nearly unrecognizable. (And not just other sports: try to explain the greatness of the movie Duck Soup without adjusting for era.) But they're still there, and they're nearly impossible to account for manually, without having to resort to sweeping generalizations like "steroid era" or juiced-ball era" to throw out entire swathes of production.

This is all to say that we should celebrate the index stat, that simple 100-based scale with such a humble aim: just to give context. It's hard to imagine how we lived without them for so long. Sabermetricians have always tried to make their stats look like other stats: True Average mapped to batting average, FIP molded to look like and compare to ERA. It's easy to understand the motivation—these statistics carry an emotional value in them that is hard to resist, as with the .300 hitter and the 2.00 ERA—but even they fall prey to the same loss of scale as their unadjusted counterparts. If a .300 average means different things in different years, does that hold true for a .300 True Average?

Instead, 100 doesn't say anything, except above average or below. And it does it instantly, for every season in every run environment for any statistic we want it to. We should have more index stats: K%+, so we can stop comparing Mike Clevinger's career 9.46 K/9 to Nolan Ryan's 9.55. HBP%+, so we can note that Ron Hunt was getting plunked when nobody else was getting plunked, as opposed to that imitator Brandon Guyer. Some might note how stale these references are and accuse league-adjustment as a backward-looking drive, and this is true. But we're always looking backward, always comparing the new with the expectations already set. The index stat just forces us to be honest.

There's always resistance to a new statistic, especially one so outwardly simple and so internally complex. We tend to stick with what we know, even in the case of formulas that are supposed to tell us what we know. But if your resistance is that it seems too complicated, too counterintuitive, too "black boxy," I encourage you to consider why you feel that way. Because the real world is infinitely more complicated than baseball, where all the pitches go in one basic direction and the baserunners are only allowed to travel in four directions. Baseball statistics based on mixed methodology are almost impossibly intricate. So are skyscrapers and automobiles. That's why we have computers—to take the guesswork out of them.

—*Patrick Dubuque is an author of Baseball Prospectus.*

Index of Names

Ballpark diagrams for Baseball Prospectus are created by THIRTY81Project, a design concept offering original ballpark artwork, including the new 'Ballparks of 2019' 11 x 17 color print.

Visit **www.thirty81project.com** for full details.

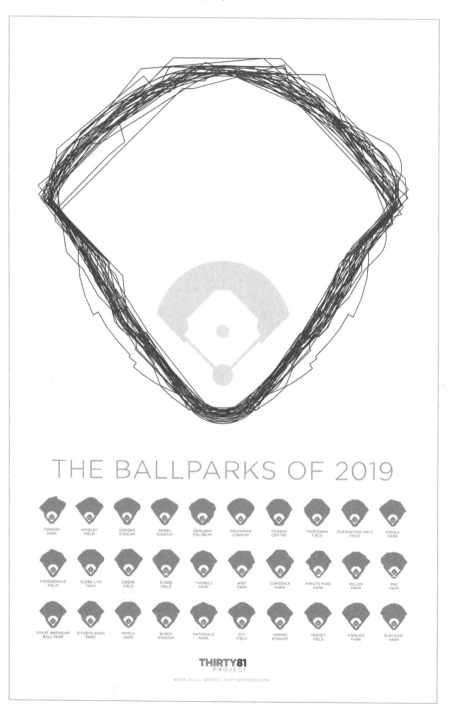